THE ROYAL ROAD TO ABUNDANT LIVING

THE ROYAL ROAD TO ABUNDANT LIVING
31 Daily Guides to Greater Health, Happiness, and Prosperity

Norah Boyd, R.Sc.F.

and

Neil A. Mence

DeVorss Publications

© 1998 Norah Boyd and Neil A. Mence

ISBN: 0-87516-720-9

Library of Congress Card Catalog Number:
98-72255

Printed in the United States of America

DeVorss & Company, *Publishers*
Box 550
Marina del Rey CA 90294-0550

CONTENTS

Foreword

It has been called the Royal Road — the road to riches, health and happiness. What is this road, how does one find it, and, more importantly, how does one stay on it?

The answers to these, and to many other questions asked by those setting out on a quest for truth, are the essence of this book.

The idea for *The Royal Road to Abundant Living*, its structure and purpose, came to me shortly after contacting Norah Boyd, a retired minister/teacher of Religious Science who taught Science of Mind in Bournemouth, England. Norah is a regular contributor of Daily Guides to *Science of Mind* magazine, published by Science of Mind Publishing in Los Angeles.

I suggested that I use material from various of her Daily Guides as a basis for developing a series of lessons to show one 'how to' walk this Royal Road. Norah readily agreed.

In preparing these lessons, the teachings of two truly outstanding Science of Mind instructors have been used extensively: that of Dr. Ernest Holmes, who founded the Science of Mind philosophy in 1927, and Dr. Raymond Charles Barker, who was for many years pastor of the First Church of Religious Science in New York City. Numerous references have also been made in this text to *The Science of Mind* textbook, which is published by G. P. Putnam's Sons. Citations adopt the abbreviation SOM followed by page and paragraph numbers, e.g. SOM 235:4.

This book contains 31 Daily Guides, or 'signposts,' that are designed to point the way and that can be used at any time. Each contains a question based on an extract from the Bible or from the writings of Ernest Holmes, an interpretation, and a meditation for the day.

I earnestly believe that all who seek spiritual enlightenment will be greatly helped by the insights and directions given in the following pages as we tread this Royal Road together.

NEIL A. MENCE
Niagara-on-the-Lake
Ontario, Canada

Introduction

The Spiritual Path is a way of life full of extraordinary possibilities for each of us. But although it brings many benefits into our lives, it is not always easy to follow without a few signposts. Once the basic rules are understood and obeyed, seeming miracles *do* happen: improved health, greater prosperity, enhanced peace of mind and more confidence are established in our daily living.

Knowing 'How To' is the secret, and that is what this book is all about. Maintaining 'right thinking,' 'right feeling,' and 'right doing' ensures that extraordinary possibilities will open up to those willing to learn and to absorb.

Readers who really want to know 'how to' reap the benefits of daily practice will discover that constant reference is made to believing. Believing is much more than intellectual acceptance; it is a conditioning of the consciousness to accept our relationship with the Giver of Life and to partake of all the bounties awaiting us.

Phrases declaring that "there is only One, in all things" are easy to say and to understand. Realizing that this also includes

you and me has to be worked on and reasoned out until a conviction of our individual divinity is so established that there is
nothing in us to deny it.

"The Father and I are One" means just that. We have a personal ego—sometimes a rebellious, wilful and self-seeking
aspect of us. We also have a deep, quiet pool of wisdom,
power, and love that stems from the 'I am' of us. This 'I am'
is the portion of God that is our inheritance. Every time we say
"I am" (anything), it is something we believe to be true for
ourselves, and our belief is *empowered BY itself*. This 'anything' that we believe in continues to express itself in our life
for as long as we believe it to be true for us. Once we realize
that we are indeed One with All Good (in potential), all we
have to do is to claim it and declare our choice to experience,
and lo and behold! "It is done unto us *as* we believe."

When followed, these Daily Guides will bring extraordinary
possibilities into our lives. It is a Royal Road that is rewarding, fulfilling, and enriching. "Seek and ye *shall* find!"

NORAH BOYD
Bournemouth
England

THE ROYAL ROAD TO ABUNDANT LIVING

Day 1

CAUSE AND EFFECT

Question. Would you please explain what is meant by cause and effect? Do I really cause the results that appear in my life—even the things I don't want?

Answer. The basic law of life is that whatever we give out, we will get back. It is the Law of Cause and Effect in action: **Whatever a person thinks and believes will manifest; whatever we ask or look for will materialize.** Whatever we sow—whether it be love, help, beauty, joy, or financial substance—as much as we give is returned to us. If we give nothing, we receive nothing. There is no way the Law can multiply nothing, for anything multiplied by nothing equals nothing.

As children, we were taught not to do things that might have harmed us. Unfortunately, this often led to our having a 'no' attitude toward life. A time comes, however, when we must grow up, not only in years but also in spiritual responsibility. If as children we absorbed a 'no' attitude, we must recognize that while it may have served us then, it almost certainly doesn't serve us now.

1

This is the time when we need to understand how our thinking works and how, through the Law of Cause and Effect, it
brings lack or abundance into our life. This knowledge is as
vital to our well-being as is proper food, education, exercise,
and hygiene. If a consistent 'no' attitude is making life difficult
for us, the time has come to change it. The 'no' attitude must
be changed to a 'yes' attitude. "Yes, what I need to do can
be done. Yes, this experience can change for the better. Yes,
I am successful in all that I do because God's love and God's
Law move through all I am!"

Raymond Charles Barker declares: "The greatest statement
one can make is, 'I am.' It is the proclamation of individuality." I wonder how many times a day we describe ourselves
with statements that begin with the words *I am*? And I wonder
how often our declaration is positive and how often negative?

Somehow we often seem to have an easier time saying: "I am
fed up," or "I am feeling bad," or "I don't have enough
money" than we do declaring: "I am happy," "I am feeling
fit and well," or "I am able to pay my bills on time." Yet every
time we begin a description of ourselves with "I am," we are,
by way of the spiritual Law of Cause and Effect, setting ourselves on the road to experience exactly that thing!

*In other words, every time we think, and believe implicitly in
that thought, we are using an immutable Law which takes that
believing thought as a direction to produce.*

We do not have to go anywhere to contact the Creative Law
of Mind. Being an aspect of God, It is always present in the
very life force of our own being. This Creative Law cannot
argue or disobey; it can only produce an effect exactly in
accordance with the demand.

Thus, every time we make an 'I am' statement, we are establishing something about ourselves through which God will express. If we say: "I am miserable," the Law of Cause and Effect validates that statement and we are miserable. But when we learn to claim habitually: "I am abundantly provided for, healthy and happy," those things are exactly what we shall be. So we are wise to be attentive when we declare "I am." For what we say we are is what, in our day-to-day lives, we shall become through the infallible operation of God's Law.

Daily we should remember that the message that Jesus brought was to trust the loving kindess of the Creator of all. When we do that, all our needs are met, and health, peace, prosperity, love, and happiness abound in our life. What more could anyone desire?

God's gifts are limitless and eternal. If we do not understand this, we could short-change ourselves. For example, someone with money, be it a few or a billion dollars, only has a *degree* of wealth, a *portion* of infinite wealth. Someone in ill-health is experiencing a small *degree* of infinite health. The secret is not to believe that a greater degree of that which *is*, is not available, but to demand an even greater *degree* of whatever good we feel we need, knowing beyond all doubt that it *is* there.

Belief activates the Law of Cause and Effect and, provided that the belief is maintained, nothing can prevent the result from coming forth.

We alone are responsible for the riches or poverty in our experience. The sooner we realize that there is *not* a God up there dispensing 'goodies' to a favored few, the sooner we

DAY 1

shall receive proof that God's love and Law are invincible and given to all alike.

Meditation

The time has come to understand the Creative Law and to use it wisely. From this moment forth I decide my needs and make my demands in absolute faith in the ability of the Law to honor my demand. As I make my claim to All Good, goodness in all ways expresses in, through, and around me. It is the proclamation of my Divine individuality. I now say "yes" to my good and I accept God's bounty with an enlightened mind and an open heart. And so it is.

Day 2

THE TRUTH ABOUT THOUGHT

Question. How does my thought affect my life? What is meant by 'habitual thought,' and why is it important?

Answer. It has been established that thought causes an effect and that we are responsible for our own thought habits and the words we speak. This is the Law of Cause and Effect —the automatic, impersonal aspect of God whch returns to us exactly what we sow into it. **Every thought believed in as true is a cause.**

A cause put into the Law will produce the effect. How important it is, then, to understand what we are doing when we think and speak! We should always remember that all of nature carries within itself seeds of its own identity. For example, a carrot can never develop from a thistle seed; a parsnip can never emerge from the seed of a tomato. Under the same law, thoughts contain seeds of like nature. Positive thoughts produce positive experiences and negative thoughts produce negative experiences.

Looking at this another way, we realize that in our daily life we are constantly using a variety of tools to cope with whatever task is at hand. These tools could be a paintbrush, a chisel, a pencil or a sewing machine. We learn to use these tools correctly to achieve a worthwhile result.

Likewise, our mind is a tool, and we need to understand its nature and how to use it to achieve the results we desire. Ernest Holmes says: "We all use the Creative Power of the Universal Mind *every time we use our own mind*" (SOM 30:2).*

Raymond Charles Barker says: "Every time we work with a fear, a worry or a doubt, we are taking the most ingenious mechanism that Creation ever produced—the mind—and using it wrongly."

The whole climate of our existence rests upon our thought patterns. The quality of our thought determines the quality of our life experiences. The greater the quantity of our wholesome and positive thought seeds, the finer our thought habits become until *habitual quality thoughts* provide a way of life producing an abundance of love, health, and happiness.

Habitual thoughts are the atmosphere of our thinking. A person who has a sunny outlook takes everything in his or her stride, refusing to take fright but confident that there is a reason for all that happens and that ultimately "everything comes together for Good." On the other hand, a person who continually dwells on the 'awfuls' of life, constantly anticipating disasters and always harping on aches and pains, is one who has cultivated a *habit* of negative thinking that colors their life and everything that occurs in it.

*See p. viii for a note on citations of *The Science of Mind* (SOM), by Ernest Holmes.

Our habitual trends can be changed, but it takes a deep desire—a constant monitoring of our approach to everything. All habits are stubborn, and it takes diligent application to change them. A good recipe is to try to be *aware*, to say to oneself: "Now, what am I thinking about this? What am I *feeling* about this?" If it is negative, change it.

For example, here in England, where the weather is a primary topic of conversation, a negative statement would be: "What dreadful weather . . . *and* it's going to get worse!" A more positive statement would be: "Well, it is seasonable, I suppose. We need rain . . . and nothing lasts forever. It will change for the better soon."

An example concerned with discussion of the weather may seem a trivial illustration but it does show that *every* event, circumstance, or experience can be a wonderful opportunity to improve our thought patterns.

In each instant we look upon that which we wish or will to look upon. God is there for the seeing; perfection is there for the seeing; light is there for the seeing. It is our ego that obstinately refuses to think, feel, or look upon the things of Spirit.

God is love and absolute forgiveness. He gives according to our capacity to receive by means of Creative Law, which we direct by the energy of our thought. Disciplining our current thought is the way to peaceful, healthy, and abundant living.

The only way to achieve a wholesome, satisfactory, and rewarding life-experience is by monitoring our thoughts and cultivating a constant, *habitually* positive, mental diet; for "whatsoever a man soweth, that shall he also reap."

DAY 2

Meditation

Freedom to think is mine. I treasure my gift of a mind with which to think. Through meditation and quiet times I form habitually confident and positive thoughts. As I carefully control my thought patterns and steer them into positive channels, I see life producing nothing but good for myself and others. The causes I sow reap rich effects, and I am forever grateful for God's love and for the truth that God is here, right now, expressing through me as peace, health, love, and abundance.

Day 3

THE LAW

Question. I have often read statements such as "God is Law" and other references to "God's Law." What is this Law?

Answer. Law means: "a rule or body of rules . . . recognized as enjoining or prohibiting certain actions" (*Pocket Oxford Dictionary*). We are all well aware of laws of nature such as the law of gravity, which keeps objects in place. There is a corresponding spiritual Law, which governs all our actions and the results of those actions. As Ernest Holmes says: "Love rules through Law. Love is the Divine Givingness; Law is the Way. . . . Love points the way and Law makes the way possible" (SOM 43:1,2).

The whole of life is giving and receiving—putting in and taking out. We are meant to receive an abundant life. We are also meant to give of what we are, to speak our word for what we want, and to receive in exact measure as we have put forth. We are not meant to take without first giving, as the Law multiplies whatever we give. Nothing multiplied is nothing. As soon as we have given something, we have crossed over from nothing to something. After that, however big our giving, we shall receive in proportion.

It is not difficult to understand God-love, for we are all able consciously to love. With God-Law, however, we may know through practice in using it that it does exist and that it does create; but we may not quite grasp what it is. Without a proper understanding of that with which we are dealing, enlightenment could be delayed.

When we desire anything enough to pray for it, we are using that Law, because prayer is simply directed and faithful thought. When people finally grasp that this Law is creative, that it is in fact the Law of Cause and Effect, they will stop misusing their thought power. Every *energized* thought power is either constructive or destructive, and everyone responsible for a cause must, through Law, reap the results of that cause.

So, going back to our example of the law of gravity, we've learned enough about it to know what we can and what we can't do with it. We know, for instance, that if we go up to a great height and jump, we shall quickly fall back to earth, perhaps with disastrous consequences. Likewise we know that without a thorough understanding of the principles of electricity, we should never tamper with it without using strict precautions. Even a little knowledge can safeguard us against disasters.

Knowledge is power; applied knowledge is protection. Properly applied, knowledge can result in health, happiness, plenty, peace, and harmony. We receive these rewards because of the time we take to study, absorb, and put into practice the basic rules governing the Creative Law of Cause and Effect. We stop dwelling on the 'awfuls' of life and concentrate on the blessings. When we apply the rules of rich and abundant living, we reap the rewards.

We are helped to stay on course when we discipline ourselves to engage in right thinking and right acting. A simple and practical way to do so is to follow the Golden Rule—to do unto others as we would have them do unto us. We need to remember that this Law works both ways, so if in the past we have suffered from our mistakes, we shall experience good according to the measure of our sense of Oneness. The good which we do is returned to us. When we stay in harmony with God's nature, we are prospered and fulfilled in every area of our life.

Through practice we learn that *God is Love*, which gives, and we learn that *God is Law*, which creates. Therefore, when we accept and cherish God's love for us and trust its givingness, and when we use God's Law and trust its creativity, all fears leave us.

At last we begin to understand that *All is Love yet All is Law*. We see that love can only give through Law, and that Law can only produce what we desire when we use it *consciously*. **It can give us nothing we do not, in one way or another, ask for.** As Ernest Holmes says: "As we gain the broader viewpoint, we shall see that Life must contain two fundamental characteristics. . . . there is an Infinite Spirit, operating through an Infinite and Immutable Law. . . . Love points the way and Law makes the way possible" (SOM 43:2).

In truth, the good we desire moves toward us the moment we use the Law correctly, but, like any seed sown in creative soil, it must go through a natural process to maturity. Abandoning our intention and falling into despair is tantamount to digging up the seed to see if it is growing. We all know that if we do that, we shall never see our desired result.

11

Patience and steadfast trust in the face of seeming delay will ensure success in the manifestation of the seeds sown in the garden of our mind. That is how the Law works. So when we pray, we must remember that the moment we sow the seed in thought, we have set the Law in motion. And as we continue to believe, we know that something is happening in the invisible and that rich and rewarding results will soon appear.

Proper use of Creative Law brings results that produce seeming miracles, which are purely the outcome of powerful direction of, and faith in, an invincible Law. Our use of God's Law and our faith in its ability to create is the only thing that produces miracles. All it takes is as much faith as a grain of mustard seed! With a tiny amount of deep conviction the Law is set in motion and miracles appear.

Meditation

I have authority over my life because I know God's Law is immutable. Somehow, in some way, my believing words and thoughts manifest perfectly at the right time and in the right place. That is the Law, and as I steadfastly trust in the operation of this Law, my patience is rewarded.

Day 4

GOD AND TRUTH

Question. We often hear the quotation from John 8:32 "And ye shall know the truth, and the truth shall make you free." What is meant by "the truth" and how does it make us "free"?

Answer. Let's start with an understanding of the basic premise upon which everything else is based: **There is only God.** This is the basis for all action, all belief, and all knowledge. In the most simple terms, the Truth is that there is only ONE. Although this ONE is known by different names — God, Father, the Great I Am, etc. — the fundamental Truth is that there is only one power, one energy, one life force in, through, around, over, under everything. For this reason, nothing can exist outside of God, since He is all. There cannot be you and God, or me and God. There can only be God being us!

We are delivered from all our fears, worries, and limitations when we seek, study, and understand Truth. Whatever we believe to be true for us is true for as long as we believe it. However, so much of what we believe has little or no foundation. This is why Ernest Holmes, Raymond Charles Barker, and all teachers of Truth have tried to alert us to the danger of false beliefs.

13

There is only one way in which we can contact God and that is through our mind—through our individual thinking. Whatever we identify with in our thinking (in other words, whatever we consciously accept) is what we become. For instance, if we identify with dressmaking, we become a dressmaker. If we identify with golfing, we become a golfer. **Identifying with anything unites us with that thing.**

We have to be aware that the ego of each of us fights to avoid domination by the 'I am' of us. The 'I am' of us is a portion of God. Just as a pail of ocean water has the same qualities (in potential) as the ocean, yet is not the whole ocean, so we are a portion of God's life (but not the whole of His life) because we are filled with God Power. So every time we say "I am" anything and believe it, that is what it becomes for us.

When we decide that we have a need, there is only one way to achieve that desire. It is recognition first that God is that object of desire and then identification with God. Since God is all there is, the 'I am' of us is already one with the great I AM. This means that we are *already* the desire. In other words, we recognize the Truth that God is all there is. We then let the Truth set us free by knowing and believing that since we, individually, are One with God, we are one with whatever we desire. It is the realization, the belief, that brings the desire into manifestation.

Let's look at an example. In a seemingly difficult situation, the desire could be for harmony, because if harmony governs any situation, it ceases to be difficult. We state believingly that "God is harmony." Knowing that we are one with God, we know we are united with God as harmony. When we realize that we are the desired harmony, the miracle happens. Harmony is demonstrated.

Another example is that God is abundance. If we desire greater prosperity, we do not need to pray or treat for prosperity but we *do* need to recognize that because we are one with God, and that since God is prosperity, we are prosperous in Truth. This Truth will manifest in our life according to the degree of our belief.

It was Ralph Waldo Emerson who said: "We must get our bloated nothingness out of the way of the divine circuits." What is this 'bloated nothingness' but our fear of lack, limitation, failure, ill-health, inadequacy—in fact, all the man-made apprehensions that stem from a sense of separation from our good?

When we eliminate our belief in separation from God, nothing hinders the Divine flow of all good into our life. Every project we embark upon we discuss with our spiritual Father, and we receive guidance. We talk about every decision we have to make with God, and we make the right choice. Whenever we need direction of any kind, we discuss it with our Inner Knower and receive the answer. We have complete confidence in the outcome of everything we undertake, because we know that we are One with our Father.

Of all the subjects we study and master to the point of success in their use, the greatest and most rewarding is the study and practice of Truth. When the understanding and acceptance of Truth has been embodied, we become a living example of someone enjoying the abundant life. The day we accept this is the day we grasp the significance of the assertion that **All is One and One is All**. There is One life, therefore we have kinship with one another and with all life.

DAY 4

This is the Truth; and by knowing (i.e. using) the Truth, we are set free.

Meditation

There is only God—one life, one love, one mind, one body, one substance, and one intelligence. As a child of God, I am one with all the attributes of God, and every moment of every day I consciously recognize and accept that God is flowing in and through everything I think, say, and do. As I accept the oneness of God, realization dawns that as God is, so am I in potential. This is the Truth about me. The Truth has set me free. Thank you, Father, for Truth. And so it is.

Day 5

THE RIGHT APPROACH
TO PRAYER

Question. What is the difference between prayer, treatment, and meditation? Is there a right way to pray or treat?

Answer. Prayer, treatment, and meditation are really one. Prayer is *not* supplication, begging, or hoping; it is a confident, positive statement of trust. This kind of prayer is called treatment.

Meditation is a quiet and calm dwelling upon our relationship with God. It is a reflection of our love and appreciation for what He is ("How Great Thou Art," as the hymn says). It is a realization of the tremendous significance that we are a part of this Wondrous Divinity; a realization that we are being loved, cherished, and provided for.

The only requirement is that we *realize our relationship*. Prayer and treatment are all wrapped up in this realization. Prayer/treatment consist of five steps. We call them steps, although each is essential in its own right—rather like the ingredients of a cake. Although each ingredient is essential, there is a correct method of use.

17

DAY 5

The five steps are:

- **recognition**
- **unification** (or **identification**)
- **realization**
- **thanksgiving**
- **release**

Recognition   We enter the recognition stage by sitting quietly, relaxing and realizing that God is the One Life everywhere present, at all times, being all things (in other words, just recognize who and what He is, such as beauty, nature, love, etc.).

Unification or Identification   Having recognized what and who God is—the Father of all—we identify ourselves with Him. We state that we are *of* Him, that we have all His qualities in potential, and that the 'I am' of us unifies with the Great 'I AM,' with His love and His creativity. Since we are always one with Him, we are Co-Creators with Him in all that we do or say. Our word is empowered with Him as Creative Law. He is, of course, both love and Law.

Realization   Having recognized God and identified (or united) with Him, we realize that because He is all there is, whatever we want to see in our life is already there in potential. So we speak our word with conviction that the degree of belief we muster in His invincibility is the Power that will stir the Law into action.

Without a deep trust and belief, spoken words are just that— spoken words—and they accomplish nothing. We must speak our word believingly.

Thanksgiving This step involves a feeling of profound gratitude that the Father's love is willing *to give* and that His Creative Law *will produce*.

Release This must not be overlooked. If we treat and continue to worry whether the prayer will be answered, it is not
released. We must let go in trust, otherwise it is like wanting
a balloon to sail away while we are still holding on to the
string. **If we don't let go, it isn't going to go anywhere.**
It remains with us.

Students often find this final step quite difficult. If worrying
and nagging doubts remain after a treatment, a good ploy is
to say: "No. I refuse to be disturbed. I have asked the Father.
I have activated the Law and I am at peace, content to wait
for the perfect outpicturing of my desire."

Jesus condensed these five steps when he said: "I thank
Thee, Father, that Thou hast heard me" and proceeded to
speak His word. Jesus had already recognized God and unified with Him. As a result, guidance was always there.

Meditation

(N.B. Today's meditation involves the five treatment steps
outlined above. In this example we are treating for a new job,
but you may wish to substitute another desire more to your
personal situation at the moment.)

1. *There is only One life; that life is God's life. It is all love,
    power, and wisdom, and it is everywhere present.*

2. *The life of God is my life now. As I unify with His love and wisdom, I am empowered to speak my word in complete confidence.*

3. *I need to be fulfilled in a new job (or _____). I speak my word that I now be guided to the job that is right for me. My talents are used to the full and appreciated. My success is certain, and I am properly remunerated. I work in harmony and peace with my colleagues and go from strength to strength under Divine Guidance.*

4. *Thank You, Father, for Your listening ear and for the perfect outcome of this treatment for the right position for me now.*

5. *My words are released to Creative Law in trust and confidence in the invincibility of God's Law, and I am at peace, content to await the perfect outcome. And so it is.*

Day 6

BEING DEFINITE

Question. How specific should I be in my treatments? For example, should I treat along the lines of saying, "All my needs are now abundantly met," or should I spell out those needs (such as a specific make of car or type of position, etc.)?

Answer. Ernest Holmes was emphatic that we should always be specific when we use the Creative Law. "Be specific in treating, be direct and definite in your mental work. You are dealing with Intelligence, so deal with It intelligently" (SOM 211:3).

Since we were made in God's image and given dominion in the world, we always have free will to decide what we would have in life. Being specific is making a statement of our desires. We must remember that although the Creative Law we use when directing our thought is intelligent enough to create, it is not in its nature to make decisions. All instructions given the Law must be quite explicit if we would have it produce our desire.

It is *not* sufficient to announce, "All my needs are met." What needs? We must be specific. Do we telephone a store and ask for groceries to be sent? What groceries? Do we go to a travel agent and ask for a ticket to the coast? Which coast? The store clerk and the travel agent will obey our instructions only if we state clearly what we want.

Several years ago my daughter and I were driving to see a movie when she suddenly said, "Mum, we haven't treated for a car space." I did a quick treatment and sure enough, there was one right outside the cinema but it wasn't big enough. I had neglected to add "one big enough for our car" in my treatment.

Having made a specific request, we release it with the words "this or something better" so as to not limit the shape or form of the good coming to us.

We then proceed to convince ourself that nothing is denied us *if* we fulfil the Law governing the manifestation of our desire. That 'fulfilment' is an unqualified belief that it *is* possible. When we fully understand that God is the Creator of all, we understand that He is the 'I AM' of us. Once we have grasped the significance of this, we then speak our word: "I am the owner of a (as much detail as possible) car," or "I am the partaker of (___) abundance," etc.

With a deep conviction that the 'I am' of us is One with the 'I AM' of God, the Creative Power within that conviction is sufficient to stir the Creative Law into action. But there must be no doubt or thought along the line of: "Well, I *hope* it will happen." There must be a complete release to allow the creativity of God to bring it forth at the right time and in the right way.

Every time we say "I am" something and believe it to be true, that 'something' comes into being. So, in fact, we are Co-Creators with God, and our part (as in everything we build) is to be specific, to detail exactly how we want the finished 'something' to be.

With many years of disbelief and a sense of loss ingrained in our habitual trend of thought, it takes perseverance, hard mental work and diligence to arrive at a state of mind that is confident, happy, and expects only good.

No power is effective without control, and thought power is no exception. When we digest this truth, we shall find proof in the answer to effective prayer/treatment work.

It can be done, and the rewards are incalculable.

Meditation

Whereas I was blind, I now see more clearly the wonders of God's provision. God has supplied all good and given me the means to declare it into manifestation. Thank you, Father-Mother God.

Day 7

ONLY BELIEVE

Question. I think that the word *believe* is over-used these days. What is the real spiritual interpretation of the word? How do we use belief, and why is it so important?

Answer. Unfortunately, many people today understand 'negatives' more fully than 'positives.' Perhaps we should look at the word *believe* in terms of *anxiety*. We all understand the emotion of anxiety. When we truly release a thought in prayer, we cease being anxious. Belief, therefore, can be interpreted as meaning the elimination of anxiety.

In *The Science of Mind* textbook we read: "The whole teaching of Jesus is to have faith and to believe. He placed a greater value on faith and belief than any individual who has ever taught spiritual truth" (SOM 450:3).

Faith, belief, conviction, trust, realization, etc., are used to describe that state of inner knowing which *knows beyond all doubt* that that to which our word or thought is directed will be acted upon by the *only* power there is. We are already one with almighty Power—our mind is part and parcel of the one Mind. To the extent that we grasp this truth, we build a foundation of faith. Our faith works for us—faith rightly placed or faith misplaced. When rightly placed, faith has no battles to fight, because situations that at one time would have frightened us are no longer seen as problems.

With all our getting, we *must* get understanding. "Trained thought is far more powerful than untrained," says Ernest Holmes (SOM 209:1). When we realize that we can speak our word and have it fulfilled, fear disappears and such a sense of security invades us that nothing can ever assail us again, because we stand upon a rock of proven faith.

If we do not have what we would like to have now, we have proved that the Law works one way, at least, because our belief that we haven't got it has outpictured as not having it. It is time to use the Creative Law in a positive direction. It works just as accurately. By properly using the Creative Law, we can receive money and rewarding opportunities; we can feel successful, happy, and satisfied, our inner mirror reflecting a perfect body with the glow of health in our eyes, hair, and skin. By rehearsing it all in our mind, a complete and perfect picture is planted in immutable Law, the mirror of life.

Belief is the key! Belief creates a channel where energy can flow. Without energy, nothing in our life can move. Raymond Charles Barker says: "The Bible is a textbook on beliefs. It is wise to remember that Jesus condensed His entire teaching into one word—*believe*. He said what you believe happens." This is because he knew that belief represents a declaration of a person's 'I am,' and 'I am' is a declaration of whatever we want to experience or be!

Nothing more simple, or more profound, could be stated. Anything of real value is profoundly simple. That appears to be a contradiction in terms but it is not.

25

The one ingredient of supreme value in making bread is yeast. Without yeast it does not become bread. A discordant chord struck on a piano can become harmonious with the addition of one or more notes. Two people in an argument can resolve their differences with a third person who introduces peace and understanding. And in prayer, the essential ingredient is belief — not just the intellectual acceptance, but a deep 'gut' conviction that the issue is certain because we are dealing with a Divine Omnipotent Principle that cannot fail. Achieving that successful ingredient is the key to successful prayer/treatment.

What marvelous simplicity! We create ideas by our thought. When the idea is sown into the fertile soil of Creative Law, it comes forth in crystalized form. Ernest Holmes says: "We are not depending upon chance but upon the Law. The responsibility of setting the Law in motion is ours, but the responsibility of making It work *is inherent in its own nature*. . . . We do not *create* the power, but we must *let* this Great Power operate through us" (SOM 305:5; 140:3). 'Through us' means through our heartfelt belief and trust in God's love and Law.

We can say that belief, which is certainty of mind, identifies a powerful inner link between the individual and the One Mind, thus establishing a connection between a person's specific thoughts and the corresponding aspects of life's essence. This activates the Law of Mind in a way that produces an exact equivalent of what one is believing.

In activating the Law of Mind, we animate it with directive awareness that brings all of the creative activity of God to bear on whatever good things we are seeking. When we decree "I am" in the certain knowledge that we are individual expressions of the Infinite, the Infinite finds a way to express Itself through us, in terms of what our inner certainty — or belief —

has established. And as our belief is more powerful, so is our demonstration more successful.

When we finally come to accept the power of a thought believed in, we shall stop declaring that we are poor, ailing, or unhappy, because we realize that those thoughts are the reasons for our experience. Changing our belief truly does change our life.

The great secret of life is to work from the inside to the outside. Believe first, because what we believe is what comes to us. That is why belief is so important.

Meditation

*The time has come for me to change my belief in the negatives and to declare the positives with conviction. My life unfolds into a miracle of goodness now that **belief**, that essential ingredient in my prayers, is entrenched.*

Day 8

DEMONSTRATION

Question. I know that demonstration means "bring into manifestation," but is it possible to demonstrate *anything* that we want?

Answer. "Jesus said unto him, 'If thou canst believe, all things are possible to him that believeth' (Mark 9:23). 'Therefore I say unto you, what things soever ye desire, when ye pray, believe that ye receive them, and ye shall have them' " (Mark 11:24).

There is an old cliché—"seeing is believing"—that is a contradiction in itself when examined. Before something can be seen, it first has to exist. Nothing can be seen until it is created. Once created, there is no question of its existence.

We all have free will, which means we can accept or reject anything. However, this doesn't mean that we are without inner guidelines for determining when certain courses of action are better than others. Truth is always available for us to call upon when we choose. Raymond Charles Barker says: "God provides food for all of us but doesn't throw it at us."

This means that Truth, though forever available, has to be recognized. Our ability to recognize Truth—and to act upon it or not—is a part of what our free will encompasses.

There is an oft-told joke that illustrates that point. A man found himself stranded by rising floodwaters. His next-door neighbor came along in a four-wheel drive offering to give him a lift to higher ground. "No, no," replied the man; "God will save me." A half-hour later the waters had risen to his waist and another neighbor came by in a boat. Again the man rejected all offers of help, saying that God would save him. When the floodwaters had forced him onto the roof of his barn, the police arrived in a helicopter, threw him a rope, and commanded him to climb. "No, no, everything is okay," called the man. "God will save me."

Well, you guessed it. The man drowned. Facing God in heaven, he cried out: "Why didn't You save me? I trusted You, and You let me drown." "What do you mean?" asked God. "I sent you a four-wheel drive, a boat, and a helicopter. What else did you want?"

While we can accept Truth or reject it, we can never escape the consequences of what we accept or reject. We create ideas by our thought. Every thought believed in as true for us becomes an experience of some kind, and that experience counsels us concerning the wisdom or foolishness of the choice we have made.

Ernest Holmes says: "We are not depending upon chance but upon the Law. The responsibility of setting the Law in motion is ours, but the responsibility of making It work *is inherent in its own nature*" (SOM 305:5).

Day 8

"And Jesus said unto them . . . If ye have faith as a grain of mustard seed, ye shall say unto this mountain, remove hence to yonder place; and it shall remove; and nothing shall be impossible unto you" (Matthew 17:20).

This shows the very essence of demonstration—faith, belief. When we recognize the two divine aspects of God—Love and Law—we know that as Love, God gives everything, and that as Law, God produces orderly, intelligent processes that correspond to our inner nature. Love provides through Law, but it is we who must choose what needs we want to have demonstrated. That choice is then fulfilled through Law, energized to the degree of our faith in that Law. Not much faith is required—only as much as a grain of mustard seed.

We understand that a powerful thought—one that is laced with an invincible belief that it can accomplish—directs unformed substance into becoming whatever the thinker decrees. Here is a scientific explanation of so-called miracles. They are simply the result of consciously directed thought filled with the energy of faith in God's immaculate Law.

When we pray "Father, give us this day our daily bread," we must accept the idea that a loving Spiritual Parent has already provided us with all we shall ever need. We recognize that the Law of God will bring into visibility whatever we have inwardly accepted. Belief is the key. Dr. Holmes says: "All doubt and fear must go and in their place must come faith and confidence" (SOM 272:2).

In other words, we must remember that we are dealing with an absolute principle that always is and that never can change its nature. We use other principles daily with complete conviction. We do not say to the principle of mathematics,

"Show me a completed sum and I will believe you can do it."
We do not say to a vacuum cleaner, "Move and vacuum the
carpet and I will believe you have the power."

In these instances and in all other principles that we use, we
first believe in the principle involved. The Law of Mind is no
exception. First believe in the principle. Give it work to do and
then experience the results. This is the only way to get a
prayer into orbit, the only way to get a demonstration. *First
believe*, and then the rest is automatic.

Meditation

*I have authority over my life to the degree that I understand
and apply Truth—the truth that Spirit provides guidance and
that every thought and desire believed by me is acted upon
by Creative Law and brought to fruition. I am free to demonstrate all the good that I can envision.*

Day 9

DEMONSTRATING SUPPLY

Question. How do I demonstrate greater supply in my life? Is it wrong to desire money?

Answer. Is it wrong to desire money? The answer is both Yes and No. The inordinate love of money is destructive but neither is money to be despised. As money is the root of world economies, a part of our everyday living, it should be handled with wisdom and recognized as a Divine Idea representing God-in-action in the business world. It should be used wisely and exchanged for goods and services lovingly and gratefully.

In *The Science of Mind* textbook we read: "No person whose entire time is spent in the contemplation of limitation can demonstrate freedom from such limitation" (SOM 267:2). And in Luke 15:31: "All that I have is thine."

It is done unto us as we believe. If we believe we are only entitled to a little, then we shall receive only a little. If we believe that we have a rich Father who is ready to give all He has, then our prosperity is assured.

It is all very well to say that we are in union with a Divine Source. We are, of course, but until we make contact we are not switched on. It is rather like a vacuum cleaner—it has the power to clean the carpet and is ready and available to do so, but until we press the switch, nothing happens. Our undoubting, invincible belief in our union with our Father is the means by which the switch is pressed. Then lo and behold! Seeming miracles happen.

What we believe about ourselves and our own wealth is communicated to everyone we meet. If we believe in our right to wealth, we emit a supreme confidence and we live joyously, happily and peacefully. Our positive attitude stimulates other people's trust in us. Hence, where doors may be closed to those who are filled with fear of lack and limitation, doors are flung wide open to those of us who feel and believe themselves to be successful.

Ernest Holmes says: "The Law is charged with the power that we give It" (SOM 396:1). How is it that we have power? From where does it come? It comes from the one Universal Spirit of which we are part and parcel. We are one with the One, and as such, we use the Creative Law by the use of our mind power.

This is an ability that must be understood and respected. Misused, this power can bring devastating results, just as the misuse of electricity can cause great harm. Our thought energy is power-full! With proper direction it can produce wonderful things. Rightly used, it can bring health, love, joy, and prosperity. As Ernest Holmes says, we all use the Creative Power of this Law every time we use our own mind.

Our responsibility, then, is to ensure that our thoughts are of the highest order, that they are constructive, loving, and directed to the end-result of prospered living for ourselves and for everyone else. If we are to achieve a rewarding life, then learning about the Science of Thought is essential.

Sometimes we need to remember just who is in charge of our lives. The answer, of course, is that *we* are. *We* are in charge of our thoughts, our behavior, our attitudes, our decisions, and our emotional expressions. No one else can do our thinking for us. No one else can control our behavior and no one else can govern our attitudes, make our decisions, or express our emotions.

When we put God above all else, we are consciously linking with Him in spirit, heart and mind. Such conscious union can have only one outcome. Every business transaction we enter into is guided by God's wisdom, every situation in which we find ourselves is harmonized by God's protection, and everyone we contact is enfolded in God's love through us.

In every area of our life we are prospered and expanded. Despite world recessions, in the face of fierce competition, and confronting seeming difficulties everywhere, we emerge unscathed with our flag of confidence in God's power flying in the strong breeze of abundance. If we want prosperity, joy, health, and happiness in our life, then an attitude of gratitude for what we have had and for all that is still to come will out-picture in outstanding prosperity in all that we are, do, and achieve.

Everyone wants to associate with a winner, and we can all be winners if we believe we are. So let us seek that new job with confidence that we are right for it and that it is right for us.

Let us pursue that ideal relationship with love in our heart, or go after that new house, knowing that it is right there waiting for us to claim it. Let us seek a greater consciousness of our unity with God in the full knowledge that as we call, we are answered.

Nothing can assail us when we put our faith in God, trusting that all our needs are met, for He responds without fail. There is only one way to discover this is true, and that is to do it.

Meditation

In love and thanksgiving I welcome prosperity into all my affairs, knowing that prosperity is God in action and that I am One with Him. In the knowledge that I am in the driver's seat of my life, I take charge and cultivate an attitude of gratitude, knowing that my thoughts are multiplied and success is assured. The results that show in my life encourage others to 'go and do likewise.' I know that only prosperity can be the outcome.

DEMONSTRATING HEALTH

Question. If I appear to be demonstrating ill health, how do I change it to demonstrate perfect health?

Answer. "For I will restore health unto thee, and I will heal thee of thy wounds, saith the Lord" (Jeremiah 30:17).

Disturbed health cannot be healed if the mind is disturbed. Humans are a trinity of being: spirit, mind, and body; and the three parts act upon each other. If the mind is in turmoil, the body reflects that turmoil. If spirit is out of tune with the Creator of all, the mind reflects the condition.

Ernest Holmes says: "Man's life, in reality, is spiritual and mental, and until his thought is healed, no form of cure will be permanent" (SOM 190:3). In everyone's life, a time for readiness to be enlightened occurs. Whether it occurs late or early is of no consequence, except that, coming early, it enables us to be healthy, happy, joyful, and peaceful, and to escape misery, ill-health, and all the attendant negatives.

Health is infinite. We may be experiencing health to a greater or less degree, but more is always within our reach, because health is the Wholeness of God, who never goes away, who never withholds His good, and who always Is.

So why do some people remain sick while others are healed? We often read that thoughts are things, and without realizing the important implication, we could ignore it. However, the simplest statement is often a profound truth. Whatever is created must first be an idea in the mind. This also includes matters related to physical health. A healthy mind will produce a healthy body. A healthy mind represents a wholesome, positive attitude to life.

While we hold on to a belief in illness, this belief will continue to register as an effect in our life. This belief must be eliminated from our mind if we are to be healed. And if we wish to help people who are suffering from illness to regain their health and to learn to trust in the Divine Healer, we must see them as spiritual beings—therefore whole, perfect and complete, rather than as merely human. We look past any outer appearances of disease and believe only in the truth of their innate perfection. We need to realize with a deep conviction that they are the essence of God and thus can never be sick.

The greatest service we can do for any person who is ill is to dwell constantly upon his Divine nature. In this way we can help him be restored to the harmony and health from which he may have temporarily strayed.

So the very first requisite for a healthy body and affairs is healthy thought. Our mind is the key to our experience, and our use of it determines our health, prosperity, and security. As Dr. Holmes says: "Thoughts of sickness can make a man sick, and thoughts of health and perfection can heal him. . . . A realization of the presence of God is the most powerful healing agency known to the mind of man" (SOM 145:3). He emphasizes this by saying that the thought that needs to be healed is the belief that we are separated from health, the belief that greater health is impossible.

"God is an immediate Presence and an immediate Experience in my mind and soul. . . . I *let* that Divine within me . . . restore me to perfect health, perfect happiness and harmony" (SOM 559:2).

How do we let it? We might want to, but perhaps we don't know how to 'let in' the health that is always ours. Perhaps we think health has to come from afar, or perhaps we have been told that we can never be cured. If so, we need to replace these beliefs with more positive ones. An example of someone who did replace them follows.

A mother suffered from 'incurable cancer' and, as a result of surgery, was paralyzed from the neck down and confined to a wheelchair. She had a little daughter whom she loved and whom she desperately wanted to care for. This beautiful child was her inspiration.

The woman rejected the pronouncement by the doctors that she would never walk again. Each day she dragged herself out of the wheelchair and forced herself to take a few steps. Gradually these increased in number until one day she told her husband what she had been doing. He began to help her, and today she continues to make progress and to tend her child.

This courageous mother rejected all thoughts of the impossible. She demanded health. Her belief that it was possible for her let the health that is the Divine Truth of her being establish itself within her.

Without doubt, thoughts are things; and healthy thoughts equal healthy bodies.

Meditation

In love and thanksgiving I refuse to believe that physical disorder is God-ordained, and I accept the health that is mine. I know that unlimited good is my Divine inheritance. As I lift my thoughts away from the things that could frighten me and center them upon wholeness, peace, and the positive aspects of life, my body reflects my sense of security in God's healing love. I open the door to health. My experience of a greater and ever greater degree of health is steadfast and sure.

Day 11

DEMONSTRATING FREEDOM

Question. I sometimes feel that everything around me is conspiring to keep my good from me. I know it is not true, but that is what the appearance is. Why do I feel this?

Answer. "We have thought that outside things controlled us, when all the time we have had that within which could have changed everything and given us freedom from bondage" (SOM 295:1).

Our ability to think and to choose is the glorious gift bestowed upon us by our loving Father. As Jesus said: "What things soever ye desire, when ye pray, believe that ye receive them and ye shall have them." In his ignorance of Truth, man has often foundered on the rocks of hatred, fear, guilt, failure, and suffering. In fact, he has sought out many ways to try to repair damage in his living experiences. Those 'ways,' so far from being the Truth, have simply built up one disaster after another.

Ernest Holmes once said: "When man is sick enough of being sick, he will get better." It would seem that disasters have a positive aspect if they drive us to seek a better way. When our eyes are opened to the Truth that our choices have perhaps been unwise and are the causes of disastrous results, we shall at last explore and examine the results of right thinking, positive approaches, and confident reliance upon a law that cannot fail—the Law of Mind.

We need to remember that because we are made in the spiritual image of God, our thoughts and words are creative. We can say: "Let there be . . ." and there *will* be. Confidence to speak our word comes from the realization that the power to accomplish is God's power and the choice of how we direct that power is ours. We decide what we want from God's 'table of bounty' and declare it into our experience.

We are in charge of our own destiny. As we come to understand the law of our own being, we also understand the power of our thought.

We are free because we can think. And since we can think, we are able to understand that our thoughts govern our actions. Thus we can decide to do something or not to do it. That which we decide to do can bind us to a situation, person, place, or thing—or it can free us. That which we decide not to do can also free us from a situation, person, place, or thing—or it can bind us.

Planting positive thought-seeds ensures a rich harvest. As Dr. Holmes says: "No person whose entire time is spent in the contemplation of limitation can demonstrate freedom from such limitation!" (SOM 267:2).

A constant turning away from unwanted conditions and demanding improvement and ultimate success in all areas recharts our journey and gives us authority over all conditions.

Recognizing and acting on this awareness ensures, not a turning away of the adverse condition, but a healing of it.

The key to freedom is belief that our thought really can stimulate the Law. When we dare to venture, when we earnestly desire to pursue this freedom, spiritual growth is assured and the Kingdom of God is ours.

The greatest gift of all bestowed upon us by our loving, spiritual Father is the ability, through the power of thought, to choose to demonstrate freedom.

Meditation

In love and thanksgiving I accept my gift of freedom. I govern my thoughts wisely, uniting them always with God's nature. I live each day consciously aware of the creativity of my thinking, and I accept in joy and gratitude the happy outcome of my disciplined and enlightneed thought processes. I am free now because I understand the Truth of my being.

Day 12

DEMONSTRATING GREATER SELF-EXPRESSION

Question. I feel that I want to do and be more, but how do I go about deciding what is right for me? How can I achieve it, and how do I use wisdom?

Answer. Wisdom and understanding come with the study of Truth. Right thinking, positive approaches to life, and confidence in our intuitive guidance all develop wisdom. The constant application of Truth develops wisdom and produces health, happiness, plenty, and confidence.

Our free will allows us to determine what we will do from moment to moment. We are able to examine options and take action that seems appropriate. We can listen to advice and decide to accept or reject it. We can travel down one road and then change our mind and travel on another road. At any moment we can seek spiritual understanding that will guide us in every area of life toward a demonstration of greater self-expression.

Most people at some time or other begin to question their reason for being, particularly when the going gets tough and a sense of despair falls upon them. Raymond Charles Barker says: "When we try to figure out why, we get into the field of doubt and speculation. Leave it to God Action."

"Now are we the sons of God" (1 John 3:2). Indeed; but we can always become more of what we already are. For example, young persons embarking upon a medical career can reach the academic finals and can call themselves doctors. Until they have practiced as doctors, however, and experienced what it means to be a doctor, they are still becoming that which they already are.

Learning to drive and passing the driving test does not make one a driver. It is the constant doing, the experience, that enables one to earn the acclaim of being a first-class driver.

Seldom are we fully satisfied with our experience. This does not suggest that we have to be poor, sick, or lonely in order to be dissatisfied. We may simply be striving in the direction of greater satisfaction, of expanding the happiness, prosperity and love we already have.

Regardless of the nature of our dissatisfaction, we can follow the same course of action in regard to improving our experience. First we must have the idea of improvement. We must develop an awareness of what we desire (often things are not so good for us, but we don't even recognize what's going on because we have become accustomed to the problem). Next we recognize that the Law of God will act on our thoughts and feeling about the matter at hand.

Do you remember the old fairy tale of Aladdin and his Magic Lamp? When he rubbed his lamp, the genie appeared and awaited instructions regarding his master's wishes. The Law of Mind is our personal genie. It is creative and produces whatever we decide we need at any given time. However, **it cannot monitor our needs or select only the good. It gives us exactly what we ask for.**

Sometimes, although we know that the condition for success is complete faith in our genie's power, exercising such faith is another matter. But if we remember the fairy tale when we call on the Law of Mind, we can look upon the Law similarly. (If we do not believe that prayer can be answered, why pray? If we do not believe in the creativity of the Law, it is useless to 'rub the lamp.')

There is no doubt that we shall 'be justified by our words,' and when those words are positive and full of faith, we lift our life above average conditions and taste the delights of a happy, healthy, and prosperous existence.

We need to realize that the whole of life is a learning experience. Just as children in school move from one grade to another, so can that process continue when we enter into the 'university of life.'

There is a trap into which we can fall if we are not careful, however. It is one of complacency and the smug conviction that we have arrived, that we no longer need to demonstrate at a higher level. Perhaps we are comfortably provided for, we have a fine home, our children are educated and launched into their careers, and we have satisfactory relationships and friends. What more could one ask for, you might wonder.

45

This is the trap. This is where we take stock and ask ourselves if we will rest on our oars or venture further to discover truth, to demonstrate more abundantly the truth that is within us. The decision is ours. The rewards that come to us in our enlightenment cannot be measured, can never be lost, and will remain with us into the next stage of existence.

Meditation

I have authority over my life because I know the truth that God is both Love and Law. As Love, God has made everything available to me; as Law, He responds to my every statement. I choose wisely though the application of my spiritual knowledge, and I demonstrate at a higher level of self-expression.

Day 13

DEMONSTRATING PEACE

Question. Attaining inner peace is probably the number one requirement to ensure a healthy and rewarding life. What steps should we take to demonstrate "the peace . . . which passes all understanding"?

Answer. "A realization of our Oneness with Omnipresence brings peace, the peace which is accompanied by a consciousness of power" (SOM 617, "Peace").

Inner peace comes from a quiet heart and a mind that refuses to believe in imperfection as a permanency. The appearance of imperfection may impinge upon our consciousness from time to time, but to remain inwardly peaceful we need to recognize that the perfection of God is present in every situation, and we need to look beyond appearances to that perfection.

Without spiritual peace, we are in a state of mental and physical fragmentation, since our mind and body reflect what we inwardly embody. Our aim, then, is to attain that fathomless peace which produces power in our living. Nothing fragmented has strength or cohesion, so we endeavor to hold fast to an awareness of our Oneness with the Divine Whole.

The realization of this Truth is our security and our strength. This is how we demonstrate peace, poise, and power— through unification with the principle of all life. Only *we* can do it for ourselves, and it has to grow.

Like any fruit, it starts as a seed and has to be nourished. The seed is sown in quietude, in silence. The seed of unification begins its growth in our meditation. "Be still and know that I am God." Think of Him, love Him, surrender to His loving care, trust Him. This is the food that nourishes the seed; this is the deep knowing that flowers into peace, poise, and power.

An aura of inner peace surrounds us. An aura of poise in a hectic world enables us to cope with anything and everything that may occur. The power that emanates from us shows that we know—and we know that we know, because we have 'been there' and are *still* there, united with Divine love.

When we use our conscious mind, it means that we are aware of, and alert to, what we are thinking. If we are not alert to the quality of the thought we are entertaining, then we shall be but 'straws in the wind': sometimes happy, sometimes healthy, sometimes depressed and ailing.

So what determines our peace of mind and the quality of our life? It is our habitual thought trends. Whatever we consciously think tends to be what we believe to be true. Remember: "It is done unto us *as* we believe." It follows, then, that to demonstrate peace, we need to heal our conscious thoughts and to hold to the thought of inner peace.

Just as God creates by contemplation in His universe, becoming the thing He makes, we create by contemplation in our personal world. Goethe tells us that whatever we want to create we must first be. Thus, if we want to demonstrate peace, we must first begin to embody the peace we desire to experience.

As we cultivate peaceful thoughts and engage in peaceful activity, that "peace . . . which passes all understanding" becomes rooted in the innermost depth of our being. Such a pool of peace wells up within us that it spreads through our consciousness out into the world and makes an impact upon people everywhere.

As Ernest Holmes says: "To daily meditate on the Perfect Life, and to daily embody the Great Ideal, is a royal road to freedom, to that 'peace which passeth understanding,' and is happiness to the soul of man" (SOM 185:2).

Meditation

In love and thanksgiving I enter into quiet meditation. I quiet my mind and heart and dwell upon the beauty that God shows Himself to be. Amidst the cool of the mountains and the warmth of the earth, I experience total peace. I share this peace with the whole world.

Day 14

SURRENDER (LET GO AND LET GOD)

Question. We often hear the expression "Let go and let God." Doesn't this mean surrender? If it does mean surrender, does it mean that we give up our individuality?

Answer. Ernest Holmes says: "Our thought becomes the thing thought of" (SOM 304:5). The thing to which we have surrendered our thought becomes power inasmuch as people who have surrendered their thought to poverty stay poor. Those who have surrendered their thought to crime are hunted and imprisoned. In fact, these people have lost their freedom. Surrendering to love, peace, harmony, etc., gives us the power to control our thinking; and when that thinking is right and constructive, we are free to live a life of health, peace, and plenty. In other words, thought of any kind is power in our lives.

"Let go and let God" means letting God do what He is infinitely capable of doing and to cease being anxious about the outcome. You *know*—because you have asked, believing in His ability and willingness to respond—that nothing can prevent a perfect result. It is only when you can pray/treat and then release all anxiety, until you have even forgotten about what you were praying for, that results will appear.

Do you remember when, as a child, you set your heart upon something you yearned for? You wished and wished so hard. Finally, when it didn't come, you lost interest and gave your attention to something else—and then Presto! it arrived! All because you had released it to the Law.

If we don't let go, the Law cannot produce, because until we do let go, we don't really believe that we have it in the invisible. This, I think, is the hardest part of a treatment (and getting it through to students by a teacher is the second hardest part).

It is only when we totally let go of that for which we are striving that results appear. Or, as Emerson said, once we get our bloated nothingness out of the way, then God can work through us unhindered.

In Proverbs 24:10 we read: "If thou faint in the day of adversity, thy strength is small." At times we all experience adversity. Such experiences can be frightening, especially if we give way to imagining the 'awfuls' that might come upon us. But Dr. Holmes says: "To desert the truth in the hour of need is to prove that we do not know the Truth" (SOM 282:4).

What is the Truth about a problem? The Truth is that no matter what the problem looks like, it doesn't have to stay that way. Out of chaos can come good—when we remember that God is ever-present. God is here, where we are, with loving provision and Spiritual Law for us to use. The most wonderful gift we have been given is the ability to think as we wish, the freedom to point our thought in any direction we choose. If we dwell upon the 'awfuls,' we shall surely get them. If we dwell upon the ability of Creative Law to make all the rough places smooth, that is what we shall get.

We learn from the Science of Mind philosophy that if we desire something, we must first believe that we have it. But if we follow our inner 'belief' with an outer struggle to get it, we are, in effect announcing a contrary belief—a belief that we don't really have it. If we really had it, no struggle would be necessary. "Know that in this Presence there is no tension, no struggle, no fear, there is no sense of conflict" (SOM 224:1).

Since God is actually in each of us, we do not have to fight to get anything; all our needs are already met. We are one with our good now. Certain processes of manifestation must occur; but what's ours is *already* ours. All we have to do is to realize this Truth and believe it. We stop trying to do it ourselves. **We let go and let God.** The Law will produce for us the external equivalent of our inner conviction.

So we can cease struggling, and what is ours will come to us. That doesn't mean that we don't need to work, but it does mean that our efforts do not have to be accompanied by misery and strain. Our work actually becomes joyful.

Raymond Charles Barker says: "God as a theological argument leads you and keeps you in the wilderness. But God as a present action right where you are, takes you where you want to go."

So-called problems have no staying-power if we withdraw the power we give them when we fearfully and anxiously dwell on them. But Law is always Law, returning to us what we are and how we think. It is always available to us and infinitely accurate in the results it brings forth, even if it creates the 'awfuls' we have imagined.

As individualizations of God, we have the power of creativity; we can do what we want to do. As creative beings immersed in the Law of Cause and Effect, we can see our creativity blossom forth. Without struggle, without fear, without a sense of conflict, all good things are ours for the declaration of them, believing.

Meditation

I have authority over my life—quietly, happily and in harmony. Whatever my desire may be, it is now in the invisible; and my word, through Law, brings it to me in fulfilment. I stop struggling. I stop trying to force things to happen. I let go and let God.

Day 15

TRUSTING AND RESTING

Question. Recently I have been going through a phase of questioning why things don't happen when I pray. As a result, I've found myself asking: "What am I doing wrong?" So my question is: "Why does it sometimes seem as though my prayers or treatments are not being answered?"

Answer. This is all tied in with our individual understanding of our relationship with God and our conviction that because we are sons and daughters of 'The Most High,' we are supplied with all our needs *when* we obey the rule of believing, trusting, and resting.

Ernest Holmes says that we are all immersed in the atmosphere of our own thinking, which is the direct result of all that we have ever said, thought, or done. This describes what is to take place in our lives. "A good tree produces good fruit, so good thoughts bear a harvest of good deeds" (SOM 448:5).

Right now, each of us is experiencing the results of our own thinking patterns. Look around and you will see it happening to others as well as to yourself. The gloomy people get gloomier, the happy people get happier, the poor get poorer and the rich get richer.

If the harvest we are experiencing is not rich, happy, healthy, and full of good-will, then it is time for a re-sowing. When our attention is given to the good sowing of rich, satisfying, and constructive seed thoughts, the harvest takes care of itself. We are free to enjoy the harvest knowing that we are indeed reaping that which we have sown.

In other words, by *believing* and *trusting* in the perfect out-come of our constructive seed thoughts, only good can appear in our life-experience. There is, however, another requirement, which is summed up in the word *resting*.

When we plant a seed, we never doubt that it will appear at the right time. For example, we plant tomato seeds knowing that with watering and weeding, tiny shoots will soon break through the earth's surface and grow toward the light. Over a matter of weeks these small shoots will grow into sturdy plants, which will ultimately bear fruit. While the seeds are in the ground, before the first signs of life have appeared on the surface, we do not keep digging them up to see if they are growing. If we did, we would never see the resulting miracle of growth.

We do not see the miracle of birth when a hen lays an egg; but we know that if the egg is placed in an incubator, a chick will appear at the right time. Whenever we 'pray aright,' some-thing starts taking place on the invisible and will appear at the right time.

We *must rest*. We *must* allow everything to appear in its own good time and refrain from constantly 'digging it up' with doubts, fears, or questions of disbelief about whether it will happen.

Our self-worth stems from the conviction and faith we have in the things that happen in nature and from knowing beyond doubt that we too are part and parcel of these wonderful manifestations. Remember that "man has been made only a little lower than the angels."

Our prayers are always answered. If we do not receive the desires of our heart, we are asking amiss. As Dr. Holmes says: "Our outlook on life must be transformed by the renewing of our mind, and even when the results are not immediately forthcoming, we must still maintain a calm serenity of thought" (SOM 218:3).

We must realize that every time we indulge in a thought that leads us away from recognizing our true nature and being aligned with what we really are inside, we remove ourselves from a feeling of unification with our inner 'I am.' Every time we embrace a positive, confident, and trusting thought, we are empowered by a recognition of our connection to that 'I am,' and we are linked to the success and well-being that is associated with all absolutes.

It is *not* sufficient to spend 15 or 20 minutes each morning in prayer or meditation and then to go out into the world leaving behind the warmth and comfort of Him who can never leave us. It is our habitual thought, our constant knowledge, understanding, and acceptance that we are One with Him that results in answered prayer. As Raymond Charles Barker says: "We can do anything we wish if we will stop scattering our energy and organize our thinking; if we will live with wisdom. Think of what you want, talk in terms of what you want, expect what you want, and act as though you had it."

Sow seeds of what you want *trustingly* into Creative Law. *Rest* and reap a glorious harvest.

We have all heard the saying "Change your thinking and change your life." That is exactly how it is accomplished. The method is infallible.

Meditation

*I have authority over my life as I recognize that I am only a thought away from all the good of the 'I am' in me. **Nothing** can come between me and my 'I am' but my own negation and fears. Each time an unwanted effect appears, or a prayer is not answered as I would wish, I am alerted to the need to change my thinking. My disciplined thought ensures that negatives are replaced by positives, and my harvest is rich indeed.*

Day 16

EFFECTIVE PRAYER

Question. It seems to me that 'prayer' is just another word for 'belief.' Is this true?

Answer. In a nutshell, 'prayer' is an *affirmation* of 'belief.' As Ernest Holmes says: "Prayer does something to the mind of the one praying. . . . We are told we must ask *believing*, if we are to receive. . . . We are to believe in ourselves because we believe in God. The two are ONE" (SOM 280:1; 435:3; 479:3). He is only repeating what we are told time and time again in the Bible: "And all things, whatsoever ye shall ask in prayer, believing, ye shall receive" (Matthew 21:22); "If thou canst believe, all things are possible to him that believeth" (Mark 9:23).

We have learned that there is a scientific approach to prayer (Day 5). Let us now look at our belief about prayer and what makes it effective.

Too often we read snippets of truth without really registering the truth that is being given. In a vague sort of way, we can read the word *believing* without fully grasping its meaning. To believe means to have such a *firm conviction* that nothing can deny it.

Although we carefully frame our prayers in specific words, the words themselves are not the key to the answer. The words only point to what they mean—the essence of thought behind the words that exists before we put any words to it. The words simply help us to clarify the desires and attitudes we bring to the prayer. Our spirit and intention are what makes our prayers powerful.

In other words, when we pray, we do not ask in hope. We express our desires in confidence and belief with conviction. The confidence comes from realizing that when we speak our word, we are using God's Law.

First, however, it is necessary to make a connection with this Almighty, Divine Power. After all, if one wanted to place an order to a supplier by telephone, just sitting quietly by the phone would achieve nothing. It is necessary to dial the number, make the connection, and then place the order, stating clearly and specifically what is required. The five steps involved have already been fully outlined (see pp. 18-19).

Belief is the essential ingredient in the process. Belief, or conviction, is thought energy; and thought energy is power. Power is the activating agency that makes things happen. In our everyday life we energize the vacuum cleaner, the electric light, or an iron by pressing a switch. Until we activate the power, nothing happens.

When we pray, we must activate the Law of Cause and Effect, and this can only be done by using our thought power—belief.

Dr. Holmes says: "There is a Power in the Universe that honors our faith in It" (SOM 32:3). When we have convinced ourselves that we can indeed trust God's Law, our trust motivates and brings forth our deep desire. Raymond Charles Barker explains why our prayers are effective or not when he says: "Until we believe a thing is, we are believing it is not." This brings us back full circle to Jesus' word: "It is done unto you as you believe." In other words, believe that something is impossible and for you it is impossible. But, believe that something is certain, and for you it is certain.

Prayer is essential to our happiness and security. Remember the story of the two little boys who were picking apples when they both fell out of the tree? One was bruised and bleeding while the other was completely unhurt. The injured boy said to his friend: "How come you're not hurt and I am?" His friend replied: "That's because I'm all prayed up."

There have been many examples of people walking away unharmed from airplane crashes, car accidents, and other disasters. We cannot, of course, know for certain that these people were in the habit of practicing regular prayer, but we do know that Something seems to have protected them.

Prayer is simply thought focused in a particular direction—a higher direction. It is an awareness of the Presence of Good in one's life. Dwelling upon this Infinite Presence enhances our sense of Oneness with It; and when we come to believe that All Good is right where we are, we greatly diminish the possibility of being harmed. We know that wherever we are in God's world, He is with us. Traveling with confidence in God's protection gives us a joyous feeling of safety at all times.

Meditation

Freedom to think is mine. Freedom to trust and believe is mine. The power of my deep desire and conviction in answered prayer brings forth my every need. I give thanks for God-love, which supplies, and for God-Law, which makes all things possible.

Day 17

FEAR

Question. What causes fear, and how can I control it? Is there any truth in the claim by orthodox religions that there is such a thing as a devil?

Answer. The word *devil* simply means false beliefs, wrong thinking, and a belief in two powers. It is the ego within that fights for domination by tempting us to forsake the positives and to embrace the negatives. Negatives are man-made, however, and can produce fear, which destroys peace of mind. When we cultivate habitual, positive trains of thought, the 'devil' becomes no more than a myth and disappears into its own nothingness.

It has been said that the entire world is suffering from one big fear—the fear that God will not answer our prayers. As Ernest Holmes says: "The fear of lack is nothing more than the belief that God does not, and will not, supply us with whatever we need. . . . But what is fear? *Nothing more nor less than the negative use of faith* . . . faith misplaced; a belief in two powers instead of One (SOM 156:3,4).

So we see that fear is nothing but a belief in two powers. On the one hand we say we believe in the power of God, but in the same breath we state: "But I don't see how He can change this situation." Well, He can't if we continue to allow our house to be divided.

Our beliefs operate upon an invincible and Spiritual Law. This Law obeys our decree because our right to choose is empowered by the power of God. What we choose, however, if not of the Absolute, is variable and subject to change. This means that belief in negatives can make us as straws in the wind.

We cannot allow fears, worries, and doubts to infiltrate our consciousness. Our teaching warns us: "Be careful what you think, because that is exactly what you will get." There are times when we must take strict control over our thoughts, our fears, and our reactions to situations. These are the times when we refuse to succumb to negative emotions. We simply cannot afford them.

We all understand the everyday meaning of committing adultery. Few of us realize, however, that we commit a form of spiritual adultery when, in our relationship with our innermost being, we desert positive attitudes and indulge in negative ones, carrying on with the 'foes' (fearful thoughts and fearful approaches such as guilt) of our own household.

Fear, unexamined and unresolved, simply connects us to more fear, which can only bring about disastrous experiences —the consequences of an inner form of adultery that, in its own way, can be every bit as harmful as the outer form. Positive thoughts, on the other hand, connect us solidly to the Creative Power of our being; and when we hold to them steadfastly and loyally, they out-picture as the ultimate answer to any apparent problem.

63

Through Science of Mind teachings we learn that all negativity is an effect and is not ultimately real. The absolute, however, is perfect, constant, and unchanging, whereas anything not ultimately real is subject to change. Fear and guilt, for example, are both human concepts, and they can be changed.

We are directed to "change your thinking and change your life." Accordingly, when we discard the unstable and inconstant negatives of our mental household and replace them with constant, unchanging positive ideas, we free ourselves from these foes. And we discover that our life becomes a happier and more joyous experience.

Raymond Charles Barker says: "A correct understanding of the Nature of God and of your relationship to Him will help you to cure yourself, because it will make you realize that when you recognize yourself as Life, you are not invoking a Power . . . you are directing Power." When we stop committing spiritual adultery, we recognize ourselves as being already united with our life source, the source of *all* Good, and we recognize that fidelity to it is our key to successful living.

All we need to do is ask ourselves one question: "Do I believe that with God all things are possible or don't I?" If we *do* believe in His Almighty Power to answer our call, then our confidence in Him dissolves all barriers.

We emerge as successful and whole human beings through a deeply felt faith in God's love and willingness to respond to our call. With all barriers removed, there is nothing to prevent God's glorious and Divine action from operating through all that we think, say, do, and become.

The rewards of positive thinking and disciplined reactions are so great, the miracle of disappearing difficulties so overwhelming, that each encounter where we overcome fear leaves us stronger, more full of courage, and more positive than ever. Why not forsake the variable and place complete trust and confidence in the one and only power that can make all things new?

Fear disappears when we center our mind on constructive thoughts, for the Law of Mind returns, exactly, the atmosphere of our thoughts. Our health, peace, prosperity, and successful living are assured when we choose aright. So let us stay with the One, never deviating, and watch seeming miracles happen. We can then say goodbye to fear!

Meditation

In love and thanksgiving I turn away from all unwanted thoughts that I have created. I live, move, and have my being in the midst of God. I am free from all fear, my inner peace is re-established, I take joy in life, and I know that only good can come to me.

Day 18

LOVE

Question. We all understand what love is when we are dealing with family and friends and the directive in John 15:7 that "ye love one another." But if God is principle, energy, vibration, how do we understand, accept, and use the love of God?

Answer. Obviously, the love that God has for us is not the kind of love we experience in human contacts. If we want peace and happiness for others, if we desire that others may find spiritual enlightenment, and if we want for others nothing but the good that we want for ourselves, then that is loving as God loves. It is a desire for someone's well-being; a desire that they feel accepted as they are, a respect for them as a fellow human being and as an expression of God within themselves. It is fulfilling Jesus' first commandment. It is a genuine, healthy, and healing love that teaches, supports, and advances the one who receives our love.

We must *never* forget about the infallibility of the Law of Cause and Effect. That which goes forth from us is always returned to us in kind and in full measure. Thus, if we want to experience love, we must give love. Ernest Holmes says: "One of the first things to do, is to love everybody. If you have not done this, begin to do so at once" (SOM 298:3). Later,

66

he says: "To know God is to love, for without love there is no knowledge of God" (SOM 368:3).

When we give love, we are uniting ourselves with our fellow human beings in a common understanding that we are each a part of the One, and we cease being suspicious, wary, or unkind toward others. Our attitude is one of friendliness, trust, and goodwill. To give love is to give freedom—not only to the person loved, but to ourselves as well.

There is no challenge in loving those who love us. The challenge is in replacing with understanding the irritation, dislike, fear, and resentment we may feel against people who we feel have hurt us. We must remember, however, that those who hurt us—perhaps by lashing out in anger—are themselves hurting inside, and usually their hurt has nothing to do with us personally. In their agony of spirit they simply need to let out pent-up feelings that eventually might harm them if not expressed.

By pouring the balm of love upon a tortured soul we help dissolve the need to hurt. When we are loving, we overcome disharmony and conflict. Indeed, love masters everything.

Too often Jesus' first commandment has been viewed with misgiving because it seems too difficult to fulfil or too restrictive to our free will. However, when we understand the value of this commandment, we realize that it is not a demand from Deity for obedience; it is for our own benefit—not God's.

He gave us this commandment out of His great love to protect us on our journey through life. It helps us to remember that "I am always here; I am constant; I am unchanging; I am utterly dependable; I will never fail you."

In Romans 8:39 we read: "Nor height, nor depth, nor any other creature shall be able to separate us from the love of God." This, taken with Dr. Holmes' statement that "Love is the Divine Givingness; Law is the Way" (SOM 43:1), shows us that nothing can separate us from the love of God or from Creative Law.

We all have life—there is only One life and that life is God. No one can be an exception, no matter who they are or what they have made of themselves. We all have access to this Divine, healing, and ever-giving love that is the essence of the life with which our spiritual Father permeates us.

We activate our connection with Creative Law through our thoughts and beliefs. What we believe to be true in any situation brings forth corresponding effects. To some this may appear daunting. In truth, though, it is most confidence-inspiring that we can choose to steer everything we are and experience into health, peace, and prosperity.

The love of God, which is part and parcel of our life, provides all the good we can imagine. Using our thinking and choosing ability to direct the Law is the *way* to enable that good to flood our being, our affairs, and our emotional security.

The Science of Mind teaching shows us how to 'pray aright.' Our prayer for others is, in fact, using God's Creative Law. Directing the Law through prayer for the benefit of all does indeed satisfy Jesus' first commandment, and the greatest reward goes to the one who satisfies that command.

Love does rule through Law. Love *does* point the way, and Law *does* make the way possible.

Meditation

*In love and thanksgiving I give right value to everything in my
life. First place goes to my Divine Father, from whom all my
good comes. I know that I attract to myself whatever I center
my thoughts of love upon. I love peace, health, abundance,
and all people. I give of myself in whatever way I can to all
who come my way. I know that, in return, I am loved beyond
measure.*

Day 19

LISTENING

Question. How does one tune in to hear the 'still small voice' within?

Answer. Ernest Holmes tells us that: "Love rules through Law. Love is the Divine Givingness; Law is the Way. . . . Love points the way and Law makes the way possible" (SOM 43:1).

It is all very well to use the Law, but how do we know that we are using it wisely? We are dealing with an intelligent and powerful force that doesn't argue with us. It cannot safeguard our interests—wisdom is not in its nature, nor is personal caring. But God-love cares. This love is ever ready to dispense wisdom; ever ready to protect us, even from ourselves, if we ask for that wisdom and that protection. When we do, then love actually influences our lives for good as we use the immutable, Creative Law under the guidance of Divine Love.

So how do we ask for love to guide us in the use of Law? Well, we ask; and then we listen—ready to sense that gentle, inner feeling of security and wise thinking. Too often we ask and then do not listen, but allow our chattering thoughts to drown out the 'still small voice.'

When we use the telephone, what do we do when waiting for a reply? Do we sit still quietly, pay attention, and listen? Or do we move about, bang a drum, or talk through any communication trying to reach us?

In our modern day-to-day living there is much noise. There are those who cannot perform their daily tasks, it seems, without a background of noise. There are those who have never experienced the renewal of soul through silence and quiet contemplation. It is as if they were afraid to allow their thoughts to become feelings. But those who have dared to indulge in deep thinking and who have opened their inner ears to that quiet and loving prompting, to ideas and guidance, have discovered a rich source of wisdom, help, and support—a haven in which to retire when the noise of the world threatens to engulf them and destroy their peace.

Dr. Holmes says that "Jesus spent much of his time communicating with his own soul. . . . [and] as the external Jesus gave way to the Divine, the human took on the Christ Spirit and became the Voice of God to humanity" (SOM 366:4; 367:3).

Jesus told us that what He did we could also do. It may take us longer to achieve complete unity with our Father, but it is not some far-off dream. With constant application, we can reap some rich fruits from Unity; but we shall never do it if we never take time to be quiet and to listen.

As we cultivate an inward consultation with a Greater Wisdom, as we seek Its advice in all matters of importance, our intuition strengthens, grows, and becomes a very real sixth sense—so much so that often 'before we call we are answered.' This guidance flashes into our awareness with such conviction that we cease to question and **we know that we know** the right action to take. It means that our door is always open.

"Let us learn to be still and let the Truth speak through us" (SOM 369:1). Dr. Holmes also says: "No man ever walks life's road alone; there is ever Another who walks with him; this is his inner Self, the undying Reality, which his personality but poorly emulates" (369:1).

At first, we often need to be quiet, relaxed, and open to 'letting the Truth through.' As we practice through meditation and habitually tune in to this Other who walks with us, we shall discover that we no longer need quietude or silence to be able to contact our Inner Reality. It is there — all the time — and because of our practice and natural turning to this Presence, we shall be able to make contact immediately, anywhere, in any situation, and in all conditions.

The moment a need appears, we shall make contact, feel that very present answer, and be able to 'let' that *wisdom* and ability through to deal with any demand that is made upon us.

What wonderful security; how at peace and confident we can be, traveling life's journey! The choice is ours to 'let go and let God' through.

Jesus was a Wayshower, and He proved His way to be a correct one! What He did, we can do when we learn to listen.

Meditation

The time has come to discover the key to a tranquil and happy journey through life. Listening to my inner reality is the key to every challenge. I use that key to open the door to love's guidance.

Day 20

PROVING THE TRUTH

Question. If all of God is present everywhere all of the time, doesn't that mean that everything we are ever manifesting, regardless of whether we call it good or bad, is in fact a manifestation of God?

Answer. Yes. It is the result of the *use* we are making of the God Power within us. "Ye shall know them by their fruits" (Matthew 7:16). "We are to know the Truth by its fruits" (SOM 436:2).

In this day and age when misery, death, and destruction relentlessly impinge upon us through the media and personal experience, we need to stay steadfastly in tune with Truth. The only answer to the many questions that arise is to be found in the knowledge of who we are.

Who we are is a portion of God Himself — sons and daughters of a Divine Father, with the right to claim our inheritance. The example of Jesus offers us guidance in discovering the kingdom as He did. "Think aright," He says, which among other things means to think positively. "Act aright," He says, which means to treat others as we want to be treated. "Love one another," He says, which doesn't mean sentimentally but rather having within our hearts a deep desire for the complete welfare not only of those we love but also of those who appear to be our enemies.

When we faithfully follow these guidelines of correct thinking, acting and loving, unbelievable good enters into our experience and we serve as examples for others.

The only way to prove the Truth is to use the Creative Law. When we use the Law correctly, everything we demand comes into our experience, and everything that comes is the fruit of our personal use of the Law. Ernest Holmes said, in effect: "Don't believe it because I tell you it is true. Go out and prove it for yourself."

Dr. Holmes says that nothing can touch us unless we let it. "Nothing is real to us unless we make it real; nothing can touch us unless we let it touch us" (SOM 307:3). We can accept anything only if we convince ourselves that we want it. When a salesman approaches us, we may at first decline to buy. When he launches his convincing sales talk, we begin to think that perhaps it would be good to buy. In fact, we 'sell' the idea to ourselves. Once we accept an idea, it manifests accordingly.

Seeking the Truth enables us to prove for ourselves that we have an invisible but immutable Law of Mind that responds to our thought direction. No matter who we are, where we have been, or whosoever we hope to be, the Law still responds. To prove the truth of anything, we must first be willing to accept its possibility. As our confidence in the invincibility of Truth strengthens, we begin to experience its fruits.

Deep inside each of us is an instinctive 'knowing' that there is good and that we ought to have it. We all seek that good.

In their ignorance, robbers, muggers, and con-men use unacceptable and unnecessary methods to obtain what they consider to be their good. The Science of Mind teaches us a better way.

By understanding that God-love has already made available all the good we could conceive of, it also shows us how to get the good we desire by use of Creative Law. We have been given a tool with which to activate this Creative Law. That tool is our thought and belief in the invincibility of God-love and God-Law. When we show forth the good fruits of our illumined thoughts, they are there for all to see. Our lifestyle gives ample verification that right use of the Law brings rich fruits to savor.

Raymond Charles Barker says: "A strong desire for a thing starts it flowing toward you." But as Dr. Holmes warns, we must be careful that our desires hurt no one — for desires that cause distress for others backfire upon the originator.

Our daily thoughts should be tuned into the love and goodness of the Infinite. No one can prosper who does not desire as much good for others as for himself or for herself. We can never outgive God; there is an infinite supply available at all times. When we prosper, we cannot possibly rob anyone else; there is enough and to spare always.

We can prove the Truth of rewarded giving by obeying the instruction in Malachi 3:10 ("Bring ye all the tithes into the storehouse, that there may be meat in mine house and prove me now . . . if I will not open you the windows of heaven and pour you out a blessing"). Tithes, in this sense, are all the positive attributes that we offer to God (love, acceptance of sonship, gratitude, right thinking and doing, a positive approach to life, etc.). In other words, give wholeheartedly, give with love, give for the sheer joy and happiness—not for possible gain—and then experience the opening of the windows of heaven and the blessings poured upon us.

To those who come into contact with us, there is evidence of our mental and feeling work. If anything is going to encourage others to seek the Truth, the fruits of our life will. So we share what we have achieved, and that can only be good, spreading the ripples far and wide to touch unknown shores.

Meditation

In love and thanksgiving I faithfully follow the way, the Truth, and the life, knowing that only better things can happen for me as well as for others when I do. Now I see that as I prove the truth, my fruits prove my own dedication. I give loving thanks for the action of Creative Law on my positive direction.

Day 21

SUCCESSFUL LIVING

Question. How is success measured? What must we do to fully live a successful life?

Answer. Everything of which we become aware has first to go through our own mind. We can look at a person quite happily until we learn that they have a terminal disease. Then we are shocked and fear-ridden for them. We can be comfortable with friends until they tell us that they have become bankrupt. Then we are embarrassed and concerned for them. Everything that affects us results from a thought in mind.

Nothing can happen to us unless it happens through us, according to Ernest Holmes. If we entertain a thought and accept it as true, then for us it becomes true, because we have allowed it to penetrate the depth of creative causation within us. If we recognize a false belief and dismiss it for the myth that it is, it has no power to express.

As Raymond Charles Barker says: ''Your only enemy is yourself, and the only thing that can hold you back is your own mind.'' Since the 'real Law' is one of freedom, we are able to make individual laws for ourselves by the use of our thoughts and feelings. The difference between 'real Law' and our own law is that 'real Law' is *Absolute*, unchanging, and forever, whereas a law we make for ourselves can be changed by us, if and when we choose to do so.

Through belief, through our habitual (and often unconscious) patterns of thought and feeling, we create and exercise authority over the circumstances of our lives. If we believe in lack, then we enter into a period of lack for as long as we believe lack to be true for us. If we believe in love, we invite love into our lives. Until we believe in the existence and accessibility of 'real Law,' we cannot confidently expect to heal problems. Perhaps, therefore, it is time for us to examine our beliefs and to change them if they are beliefs in the negative.

Let's look at this another way: a man deciding to build a house first decides upon the quantity and quality of bricks he will use and then estimates how much time and effort will be required. When we decide to build a tower of strength so that our whole thinking structure withstands any kind of negative battering, we must first calculate how we can ensure that each 'thought brick' we use passes the test.

Dr. Barker tells us that: "Casual negative thinking does not cause serious sickness. A negative repeated until it is subconscious causes serious sickness." Every 'thought brick' we make to use for our tower of strength must be laced with faith in God, belief in His ability to make all things new, and trust in His abiding love to guide us at all times. Dr. Barker also says: "This teaching [the Science of Mind] puts you in the driver's seat. You do two things: think and feel. These two things are the Creative Power of existence."

Dr. Holmes tells us that "Faith is built up from belief, acceptance and trust. Whenever anything enters our thought which destroys, in any degree, one of these attitudes, to that extent faith is weakened" (SOM 159:1).

Constant vigilance and persistence is the key to successful building, and after a short time we discover that positive and faith-provoking thought habits become increasingly easy and we can take refuge in our own tower of strength. Thus the constant tendency of our thought is the determining factor in successful living.

Cultivating habitual, positive, and constructive attitudes to life can be a seemingly formidable task. Many of us have cultivated the very opposite over the years simply because we have not known the truth. It is never too late to change. As Dr. Holmes says: "If the visible effect in our lives is not what it should be, if we are unhappy, sick and poverty stricken, we know the remedy. The Truth is always the remedy, and the Truth *is* that the law of liberty is the only real law. When we reverse the process of thought, the effect will be reversed" (SOM 483:5).

Imagine wanting to drive a stake into rock-hard earth. What must one do? Surely, the only thing to do is to strike the stake again and again until the earth gives way and receives the stake. Continual bombardment finally achieves success. Our subconscious can be likened to rock-hard earth. Truth can eventually be hammered in—and then what have we? A subconscious that holds Truth as firmly as it once did the negatives.

Dr. Holmes says: "Through constantly applying ourselves to the Truth, we gradually increase in wisdom and understanding" (SOM 271:4). So what does this acquisition of wisdom do for us? Many times in the Bible we are told that wisdom is more precious than gold, silver, or jewels. Why? Applied wisdom means control of our own life. With an understanding of God's Love and Law we deepen our faith and trust, which banishes fear. We achieve a peace of mind and a sense of security that no amount of material possessions could provide, for these are things that come and go and that eventually pass away. God's Love and Law are forever! When we accept God's Love and use His Law with knowledge, the inestimable Truth begins to dawn, and wisdom takes up its abode within us.

Constant application of the Truth is the way to acquire wisdom. A persistent positive tendency of thought is the key to successful living. By it and through it we become healthy, wealthy, and wise.

Meditation

Freedom to think is mine. In love and thanksgiving I monitor my thoughts, and the strength of my belief in the reality of a thought governs my experiences. By right thinking I align myself with good. By right thinking I properly use Creative Law. My success is guaranteed.

Day 22

POWER

Question. We know that God is both Power and All-Powerful. How do we use this Power to improve the quality of our lives?

Answer. What do we understand 'power' to be? We are not talking about a degree of superiority whereby one person might have power over another, or one nation could be stronger and mightier than another. The power we are dealing with here is a life energy; something that impels, accomplishes, and creates.

The Bible has many references to the power we have been given. "Behold, I give unto you power . . . and nothing shall by any means hurt you" (Luke 10:19). "For God hath not given us the spirit of fear but of power and of love and of a sound mind" (2 Timothy 1:7). And in the *Science of Mind* textbook we read: "Until we awake to the fact that we are One in nature with God, we shall not find the way of life. Until we realize that our own word has the power of life, we will not see clearly" (SOM 145:4).

Ernest Holmes says: "The Law is charged with the Power that we give It." How is it that we have power? From where does it come? It comes from the one Universal Spirit, of which we are part and parcel. We are one with the One and, as such, use the Creative Law by the use of our mind power. Of ourselves we can do nothing. It is only as we unite with power—life power—that we can be powerful. Only as we move near to that Creative Power can we become a partaker of power.

We live, move, and have our being in an ocean of love and Law—with God being both. Because of this, we inherit individualized God power. As God creates on the universal scale, so we create in our own lives. Every time we think, believing our thought to be true, something appears in form through Law. This is our individual use of the One Universal Power.

Realizing that there is a Creative Law, and then using our thought to activate that Law in a direction of our choosing, is how we can consciously create happy and satisfying circumstances in our lives. When we believe that the Law's response to us is as predictable as any other law of nature, and that nothing can stop its action (other than our own change of thought to something that contradicts our prior belief), then we can successfully use the Power at the heart of the Universe.

The secret of becoming full of power is in the acceptance that it is there, waiting to pour through us. Walter Lanyon states in one of his books: "When you are ready to stop this ridiculous praying to a man-made God, and come before the Presence with the glorious readiness to let the power into expression, then will you see and know, 'the words I speak are not of myself but of Him that sent me.'"

In other words, by our acceptance of the Presence, and therefore the Power, we have united with it. Emerson understood this when he declared: "We must get our bloated nothingness out of the way of the divine circuits."

What could anyone want other than power, love, and a sound mind? All of these things bring confidence, happiness, and an enriched life. No matter what condition might prevail in our life experiences today, we can, with a deeper understanding of our relationship to God, change adversity to enrichment while keeping, without fear, the good we already have.

Love is powerful in our life because as we give it unconditionally, it is returned to us in like measure. Not the false, selfish emotion that is mistaken for love, but a healing, promoting, and caring givingness that blesses the giver and the receiver.

A sound mind allows us to embrace the simplicity of Jesus' teachings. "As we sow, so shall we reap," he says. When we sow thoughts and attitudes of love, caring, and giving, we are bestowing qualities inherent in our nature, because those qualities are in the Divine Nature of God. Exercising those qualities activates the Creative Law of Mind. Therefore love works through Law to bring experiences in like measure to both the giver and the recipient.

What do you want more of? Love? Then give more. Money? Then give more. Success in business? Then promote greater business for others. Anything given with love is rewarded by increase.

So we pray with an expectancy of perfect results, improved health, greater wealth, more peace of mind, more harmonious relationships, a better job, a new home or car, or anything else we need at the moment. We can expect change to occur along the lines of our prayer. Change is what we shall get when we direct the Law with conviction.

Meditation

Now I see that because I recognize and accept the One Power filling all that I am, my thought directs the Creative Law. I have greater authority over my life as I understand to an ever-increasing degree the power I use when I pray for my needs to be met. I speak my word with confidence and rejoice that I now see more clearly. The time has come for me to give, give, and give yet again, and so allow the nature of God within me to be fulfilled. As I sow, so shall I reap.

Day 23

MY WORD

Question. How is it that my word has power?

Answer. In Isaiah 55:11 we read: "So shall my word be that goeth forth out of my mouth. It shall not return to me void." Ernest Holmes says: "Until we realize that our own word has the power of life, we will not see clearly" (SOM 145:4).

He also says: "Since our spiritual understanding is not [yet] sufficient to enable us to mentally set bones, we call in a surgeon; since we cannot [yet] walk on the water, we take a boat. We can go only as far as our spiritual knowledge takes us" (SOM 219:2). However, this is no reason to mark time at our present level of knowledge. There comes a time when we must generate faith in the invisible things, for such is eternity.

"Words carry the mind forward to a place in thought where realization begins," Dr. Holmes says (SOM 409:5). Where realization begins to dawn, learning is increased and we are carried forward to greater understanding, deeper wisdom, and a peace that can only come through conviction and reliance upon the unseen realities.

When we speak our word, how convinced are we that it will be effective? Do we fully understand what makes it effective?

Confidence is built upon understanding. To skate or ski or drive a motorcar successfully, certain techniques must be understood and applied. In fact, to achieve a perfect result in anything, we must understand a set of basic rules and apply them.

Speaking our word in full confidence of the perfect outcome is no exception. **Too many people think that speaking a scientific treatment in a given formula is sufficient. It is not, as the ineffectiveness proves.**

Dr. Holmes reminds us that man has the same power in his own life and in his own world as has God in the Universe. And so he does when he understands what that power is.

Since we are united with the whole of life—life that is God—our word can become the thing unto which it is sent, but only if that word is empowered with invincible belief that it *is* filled with God-Power. This is the result of our conditioned consciousness.

When we speak our word, it must be filled with the awareness that 'of ourselves we are nothing' but that united with God-Power we are everything. We have been given dominion; it is our choice whether we take that dominion—but it has to be earned. It has to be paid for in spiritual coin.

God is our Spiritual Parent and we are parents of our biological children, or those we have care of. What happens when our children or charges say: "I want . . ." or "Can I have . . ." or "I need . . ."?

As loving guardians we do our utmost to satisfy these requests. If the children do not ask, their needs and desires go unmet. We cannot *be* parents or guardians if we are denied the opportunity to supply.

In exactly the same way, we have to ask our Spiritual Parent for whatever we want demonstrated in our lives. Since we all have free will, it is incumbent upon each of us to choose what we want at any one point in time. If we don't ask, we cannot receive. This is why we are told: "Ask and it shall be given unto you; seek and ye shall find; knock and it shall be opened unto you" (Matthew 7:7). "Let your requests be made known unto God" (Phil. 4:6).

Isaiah, in his complete understanding of speaking his word, and his supreme trust in the certainty of a Divine Response, said: "So shall my word be that goeth forth out of my mouth. It shall not return to me void."

So we must remember not only to ask God for what we want, but also to imbue the asking with utter confidence that the answer will be complete, successful, and perfectly satisfactory.

Meditation

The time has come for me to apply my heart, mind, and intuition to understanding the God-Power that can energize my spoken word. My belief and conviction, which fills my consciousness, brings perfect results now.

Day 24

AN 'I HAVE' CONSCIOUSNESS

Question. A friend was four months behind in his car payments, and although he treated and treated for a miracle, he ended up losing the car when the bank took it. Why did this happen?

Answer. First, we must understand, believe, and accept that since God is *all* there is, there can be no such thing as loss or lack. It is a question of either an 'I have' consciousness or an 'I have not' consciousness. There must be a total understanding and acceptance of the statement "For whosoever hath [in consciousness], to him shall be given and he shall have more abundantly. But to whosoever hath not [in consciousness], from him shall be taken away even that he hath" (Matthew 13:12).

This passage in Matthew has caused many people to puzzle over and query the truth of it. After all, it hardly seems fair that those who already have plenty should receive more, whereas the people in lack lose what little they may have. Like many lessons in the Bible, the phrase has to be understood from a spiritual viewpoint.

Let us try to grasp the true meaning of 'having.' This kind of having means an innner conviction that something is yours, a conviction that cannot be shaken, because you know—and you know that you know.

Suppose you received an authentic letter from a lawyer saying that an inheritance of great wealth was yours. Not only would you be overjoyed, but no one could tell you it wasn't true! Your conviction would mean that you had it in consciousness, even if not actually in your hand yet. To him that hath (in consciousness) more will be given. The belief (in consciousness) of having stimulates greater prosperity.

The Science of Mind teaches that no condition is unchangeable, no circumstance is more powerful than Truth. A difficult situation is just a reminder that it can be changed into a better situation. "Judge not according to appearance, but judge righteous judgement" (John 7:24), we are advised. Appearances last only to the extent that we accept them as real and entertain them in mind.

If we see a negative situation as an appearance rather than as Truth and turn away, resisting the temptation to pay it attention, we literally starve it of its power to survive. Only by steadfastly dwelling on perfection can we begin to eliminate those unwanted appearances brought about through our own invention. Maintaining an 'I have' consciousness is a sure-fire way to permanent prosperity.

From stories in the Bible we can learn how to overcome seemingly insurmountable difficulties. Whenever we feel threatened in any situation we would do well to study and absorb the lesson of David and Goliath.

Whenever fear paralyzes us in the contemplation of the enormity of a problem, the story of David's faith will show us how to overcome that fear and win through. Just imagine: here was a great hulk of a man armed to the teeth ready to do battle with David, armed with just a stone! When we meet a problem as big as Goliath and direct our stone of Truth at it, how can we miss with such a big target? The bigger the challenge, the more certain we are of hitting it.

Raymond Charles Barker says: "When we cross out our negatives and let them die, everything separating us from God is removed." Ernest Holmes says: "With God all things are possible. . . . [but] this Power of God must be hooked up with our thought" (SOM 315:3).

So if we are sick, unhappy, poverty-stricken, or in fear of loss of anything at all, we desert the negative thoughts and direct our belief in the Almightiness of God-Truth to the very heart of the problem and watch it disappear into its own nothingness. Every day we have opportunities to prove that holding fast to the Truth does indeed bring harmony into any situation. Every day those opportunities strengthen our faith in God's love and God's Creative Law.

If you feel enmeshed in negative happenings; if you feel any kind of lack—be it in the areas of health, finance, domestic affairs, suitable employment, or anything else at all—all you have to do is to remember: "Make your requests known unto me" and "Ask and it shall be done unto you."

Then do this: First, be clear and specific about what you want to experience (and careful to frame your thinking around what you *do* want and not around what you *don't* want). Then, as you 'make your requests known,' believe that Almighty God and Invincible Law will respond with exactly what you want to experience. This is using your power to think and to act; and Creative Law can never fail to deliver.

When we *'have'* in consciousness, we are truly united with All-Abundance and cease to keep demanding it. After all, does a millionaire worry himself to distraction about where his next penny will come from? He *knows* that he has sufficient for his needs.

Jesus said: "It is done unto you as you believe." The more we can accept in consciousness of God's abundance, the more of it we shall experience. Always, what we truly believe is what we shall get. The abundant life is as near as our positive belief.

Meditation

I have authority over my life because I recognize the problem of having unwanted beliefs and negative thoughts. I now use Truth as it is intended to be used and know that nothing but Good can attend me. I have a consciousness of having, and nothing can limit or obstruct the reflection of this belief in my life. I am secure in God's Presence and Power, now and always.

Day 25

I AM WORTHY

Question. If my prayers are not being answered, does it mean that I am harboring a feeling of not being worthy?

Answer. From the Bible we have the assurance that "As a man thinketh in his heart, so is he." There is no doubt that realizing the link between heart and mind is of the utmost importance. A heart and mind in disunity bring nothing but chaos in a life. Chaos in any shape or form says goodbye to control. No one can move in opposite directions at any given time, so when we lose control of our heart and mind, we lose control of our good experiences.

It would seem that the biggest hurdle that many people have to overcome is a feeling of not being worthy to have prayers for themselves answered. Many times we successfully pray for others, but prayers for ourselves often fail. Why? One possible explanation is that while we can readily understand that other people are cherished by a loving Father, we cannot fully believe that we also are loved. It is essential that such feelings and thoughts be abandoned and that we accept that we are just as much cherished by our Father as are all His other offspring.

If we want to live a happy and rewarding life, we must be diligent in keeping what we think in unity with what we feel. No number of mental statements that we believe in the Almighty Power of God-Law will produce a harmonious solution unless our heart is in agreement with what we think. This is the mystical marriage. This is the means by which we keep control of the happenings in our life and realize our worthiness.

Jesus is a wonderful example for us to follow. He accepted his authority to speak His word and to have it happen. He told us that we could do the same. All it takes is for us to realize with a deep conviction that Divine Power is available and then to unify with It—in other words, to accept that It is One with us and that we are One with It. We should then recognize that we are always heard and that we are ''then filled with authority'' as we make a claim for whatever we desire, knowing that *with that authority* the Creative Law must obey.

What we believe to be true in heart and mind is what we experience. It follows then that we must obey the command in Proverbs 4:23: ''Keep thy heart with all diligence; for out of it are the issues of life.''

Raymond Charles Barker advises: ''Watch your mind. . . . You cannot afford the luxury of negative thinking. The price is too high and the results too certain.'' There, in a nutshell, is the answer to lack of confidence and to a belief in being unworthy.

When our thoughts are positive and our trust in right action is firm; when we go forth knowing that we cannot be where God is not; then confidence takes possession of us and we can go forth to achieve, to accomplish, and to prove that with God (i.e. being in tune with God's will) nothing is impossible. Hand-in-hand with confidence comes a belief in being worthy.

Knowing that we are worthy, keeping our faith in the Almighty Power and Presence where we are, believing only in the good, and accepting wholeness and its availability to us ensures perfect control and perfect outpicturing of the issues of a heart and mind in agreement.

Jesus taught by personal knowledge and example. "Look," he said, in effect; "It is not only possible to achieve results from your spoken word but, if you truly feel united with the Presence, the results are certain." We should grasp that gift of authority with thanksgiving.

"It has taken humanity thousands of years to learn that it has the power to control its own destiny" (SOM 137:1).

Meditation

Freedom to think is mine. I constantly monitor my thoughts and feelings to keep them in accord with harmony. This means that I am in perfect control of my life-experiences. I now discard false humility and realize my true worth to my Divine Father. He has given me authority, and I use it for good and in thanksgiving. My belief in the Presence and Power of God in my life gives me confidence and an understanding of my unique worthiness.

Day 26

OUR ROLE

Question. We have learned the Truth that God the Good is All there Is. What is my role? Is it to sit quietly and to let Him operate through me, or is there something I should be doing?

Answer. In the Gospel according to Matthew we are told in a very concise way what our role in life is: "But seek ye first the kingdom of God, and his righteousness; and all these things shall be added unto you" (Matthew 6:33).

Jesus told us that the kingdom of God was the kingdom of the soul and that whatever tends to purify in thought, word, and deed will cleanse the temple of the flesh. This means that a cleansing of our inner and outer being is summed up in the concept of unconditional love. Love has a healing quality, and when we truly love and accept others as we would be accepted, we are cleansed inside. Our spirit is united with the Holy Spirit, and we indeed find the kingdom of the soul.

Through our teaching we understand the action of cause and effect. Putting a new cause of unconditional love into our innermost being produces an outer effect beyond our wildest dreams. Finding the kingdom takes perseverance and dedication.

Each of us finds many pathways presented to us during our lifetime. Our choices could result in disaster or spiritual maturity, ill-health and failure or a peaceful, happy, and carefree existence.

In facing our own particular challenges we would do well to heed the lesson of poor old Job, who was beset by many negative experiences until he finally became wise. He tells us: "Acquaint now thyself with Him and be at peace" (Job 22:21). When we acquaint ourselves with anything, we become that thing. Who better, then, to acquaint ourselves with than the Divine Being? When we study God, we become more Godlike and therefore more imbued with the qualities that form the nature of God: peace, wisdom, joy, love, and abundance.

We are told by Raymond Charles Barker that "The more we dare to be spiritual, the more we minimize potential trouble." Why? Isn't it because by following the spiritual pathway, we lead orderly, secure, and confident lives? He also advises: "We should take time every morning to do our daily specific mental work. It is the only way there is to maintain a control over the floodgates of the universal subconscious mind so that negatives cannot enter."

He also says: "No one has ever gone forward by looking backward." The only time we can live is now! We cannot live yesterday: it has gone. We cannot yet live tomorrow. Jesus said: "Follow me and let the dead bury their dead" (Matthew 8:22). While we keep hold of the dead past, we remain dead to any hope of a bright and glorious future.

Jesus also makes it quite clear what we must do when we are anxious, worried, or concerned about other people. He says: "What is that to thee? Follow thou me."

So what happens when we do follow him? Immediately we cease to dwell on the problem we think envelops another, so we stop putting ideas into mind and making a law for them. Then, when we realize the truth that God is far better able to take care of them than we are, our own conflict disappears.

In advising how best to practice using the Science of Mind, Dr. Barker says: "Take what you are and use it more wisely." This points to a powerful and important truth: we do not need to get anything else or be anything more. We simply take what we already are and use it more wisely. Doing so is the 'Way' of which Jesus speaks.

Spiritual truth has always been available, but we shall not see it until we open the shutters of our mind. For too long our vision has been limited by our own limitation and ignorance, and we have been unaware of the exciting discoveries to be made —whether personal things or the wonders of the Universe.

The Science of Mind teaches the ultimate reality of the invisible and the changeableness of the visible. Though the relative is in a constant state of change, the Absolute never changes. This Absolute part of us is our Divine essence, our pure God-nature, and it needs no improvement, for it is already the best of everything. It can, however, always be applied with more wisdom, more understanding, more compassion. Grasping this fundamental fact, which is the basis of all constructive change, requires study, dedication, enthusiasm, and application.

If we need to change any condition, we first recognize that it is relative, which means that change is possible; we're not stuck forever with anything. Having recognized this fact, we now use the Law of Mind as a tool to fashion new conditions. This Law is dependable, secure, and efficient. We can safely put our trust in it—even as we trust the love of God—and then realign our thoughts and feeling so as to bring into our experience the 'Life Abundant' that Jesus tried in so many ways, through so many stories and precepts, to help us understand.

Meditation

I have authority over my life. Freedom to think is mine, and every day I take time to withdraw from the relative and enter the Absolute. My constant direction to God-Law ensures that I experience stability, success, and peace. In love and thanksgiving I emerge stronger, more at peace, and wiser. Health and plenty are mine, and I am greatly blessed. Thank you, Father.

Day 27

FEELING THE PRESENCE

Question. What is the best way to overcome a problem? For many of us, it is one thing to sit and meditate or to read *The Science of Mind* and positive literature like that. It's quite another thing, however, to go out into the world and face challenges such as unemployment, ill health, or financial lack, etc.

Answer. In the beginning, God gave man dominion over everything; man could *name* everything that is. In our every-day experiences we have the opportunity to name something as 'good' or as 'not good.' Whatever we name it, that is what it becomes for us, because that is what we believe about it.

For example, a negative person loses his or her job and names it bad, while a positive person names it a good opportunity to find something better. A person plunged into bankruptcy can name it a disaster or look for the reason, declaring that he or she is being freed for a wonderful, enriching experience. When one can trust Good to dominate one's life, no matter what the appearance may seemingly be, that person is re-warded because of their belief in the ultimate benefit that the positive naming of an experience brings. Challenges well met make one strong mentally, emotionally, and spiritually!

Ernest Holmes says: "We cannot live a choiceless life. Every day, every moment, every second, there is a choice. If it were not so we would not be individuals. We have the right to choose what we wish to experience. We have the right to choose the kind of companions with whom we wish to associate; to say in what city and in what type of house we would like to live" (SOM 143:3).

We must constantly be aware of our *habitual* thought. We must constantly be on guard to ensure that doubts, fears, and anxiety do not creep into our minds. To do this, we turn away from all negative appearances, we 'Let Go and Let God' by knowing the Truth and living the Truth. In other words, we put into practice what these Daily Guides teach us.

If we have a sense of loss or lack, we shall experience even more loss and lack. This is the Law obeying our belief. The Law works by appearing not to work. It isn't easy; it requires constant vigilance. But, if we are to lead a life full of health, happiness and prosperity, we must constantly choose our thoughts wisely, believing in the ability of God-Law to satisfy our desires.

Dr. Holmes says: "A realization of the Presence of God is the most powerful healing agency known to the mind of man" (SOM 145:3). To realize this Presence, to actually *feel* It, we must condition our consciousness.

To obtain a result for anything, certain rules or conditions must be fulfilled. To develop a negative, a darkroom is essential. For music, we must have instruments or a human voice.

To measure anything, we must employ arithmetic. To obtain silence, we must stop talking. Just so with spiritual matters: our consciousness or state of mind must be conditioned to become aware of the Presence.

Too many people think that using certain words in prayer/treatment work is sufficient. They are not, and those people are usually confused and disheartened when their prayers are not fulfilled. We must remember that it is not words alone that stir the Creative Law; it is the depth of feeling that accompanies the words—the belief in the invincibility of the Law that empowers the words. Results will appear when a person can treat and then release all anxiety about that for which he or she is praying.

The whole purpose of meditation, the significance of unifying or identifying with God, is to establish an awareness of this loving Presence. ''Be still and *know* that I am God'' shows us how to achieve this unity. We quietly and firmly discard all extraneous thought, and, as the silence enters our being, the Presence makes Itself felt. We need to fully understand the meaning of God as '*THAT* I AM,' as well as the 'meaning' of ourselves, when we declare ourselves to be anything.

Since Jesus was so evolved, he was permanently united with the Great 'I AM.' Whenever he referred to 'I AM,' he was meaning '*THAT* I AM' which is the principle of all life. It is the 'that' of everything. When God knows Himself as anything, 'that' becomes the thing. This means that whenever we declare ''I am'' anything, it becomes that thing for us because we are of God. When we declare (and believe that it is possible), ''I am healthy, prospered, loved, happy. . . .'' that is what it becomes for us. So we too are '*THAT* I AM,' but to a lesser degree.

In reality, God is the 'THAT' of *all* things; we are the 'that' of our human experience.

This experience is available to all who persevere (without anxiety) to achieve a conditioned consciousness. The secret is to gently fill our heart and mind exclusively with loving God and to trust and to have confidence in Him. The Presence responds in full measure.

Meditation

The time has come for me to practice feeling the Presence. I now choose my thoughts carefully and think and demand only those things that will prosper me. As I open my heart and mind to the quiet realization and acceptance of Divine love, that Presence fills my whole world, and I am at peace.

103

Day 28

JOY AND GRATITUDE

Question. Someone said that "joy is the strength of the Lord." How does this tie in with practicing the Presence and being thankful?

Answer. " 'In everything give thanks.' An attitude of gratitude is most salutary, and bespeaks the realization that we are *now* in heaven" (SOM 497:2).

Most people have known joy at some time in their life—joy at discovering human love, joy at the birth of a precious child, joy when a loved one recovers from a serious illness. So why are we not more joyful every moment of every day? Why is joy in less evidence than worry, fear, poverty, and loss? If allowed to remain, all the negatives in our life would deprive us of the elation and thanksgiving that should dominate our lives. Raymond Charles Barker says: "Everything that is wrong with you is a conditioning of the past. And everything that is right is a potential for the future."

Since we are thinking individuals, responsible for our own thoughts and beliefs, the conditioning that brought forth the negatives must be of our own making. We can change our thought patterns and bring forth positive and joyful experiences, but we must first wake up and become aware of our negative trends. Paul says in Romans 12:2: "Be not conformed to this world, but be ye transformed by the renewing of your mind." Here is a clear message on how to cast off the past and to enjoy the kind of life we are meant to experience.

If we were driving along and suddenly realized that we were on the wrong road to our destination, what would we do? Exactly! We would stop, look at the map, get our bearings, find where we went wrong, turn around, find the right road, and then proceed in confidence, knowing that we would soon reach our destination.

Our life is a journey—a journey toward the goal of unity with all the Good that awaits us. If we examine our trend of thought, if we make an effort to change our negative patterns to the positives, we shall be taking steps to put ourselves back on the right road. Our whole life situation would be changed and the resulting peace, health, happiness, and plenty would cause us to leap in joy! Joy in the glorious liberty that union with our Father would undoubtedly bring. The moment to turn around is *now*.

The right path has been shown us, and as we become stronger and more confident, that joy remains with us and we are truly grateful. When we are grateful for anything, however small, it expresses a belief in Good. A belief in Good promotes more Good to flow into our experience. Moreover, when we give thanks for anything, we are in fact believing that we *have* that something. No one gives thanks for something that they don't believe they have. "Believe that thou hast and more will be given."

Many people would query the last part of the quotation from *The Science of Mind* given at the head of this Daily Guide. Few would agree that "we are now in heaven." Within them would rise up denials such as: "What about my failing business?" "What about my ill-health?" "What about my quarrels with the family?" Notice that many people claim their negatives by using the word *my*. They believe that these negatives are theirs. The Law of Cause and Effect is that anything we believe to be ours becomes our experience.

Most of us have heard of the little fish that asked of its mother, "Mama, what is water?" Replied mama, "I don't know!" We live in an ocean of love, we have our being in Divine Love and Creative Law. The very breath we breathe is by courtesy of God's love; every result from every thought is by and through God's Creative Law. Of course we are now in heaven; but we are not aware of it.

It is a well-known truism that the teacher, usually much more so than the student, benefits from the lesson being taught. Likewise, anyone giving service to another is often benefited more greatly than the one served.

For example, when we act as peacemakers and restore harmony in a situation, that harmony becomes more fully expressed in our own personality. And whenever we pray for strength for another, we too are strengthened.

The reason for this is that in the act of convincing ourselves that God's perfection is the Truth of the individuals concerned, our consciousness becomes deeply engraved with the idea of our own Divine perfection. When we declare the Truth about another, our own belief in God's constant Presence with all persons is deepened, and we are uplifted.

Sometimes, in offering our gratitude to God for the many blessings we have, we forget that words of gratitude are not really enough. The way we can best express our gratitude is by caring for another, by supporting him or her when there is a need, and by sharing what we have. Then, indeed, shall we be living our knowledge of Truth.

When we realize the gifts we have been given, and when we utilize those gifts to make our life heaven-upon-earth, we shall indeed feel overwhelming gratitude rising up from within us! "Oh how grateful I am, Father-Mother God, for your life and love that is expressed as me! Oh how I love thy law!"

Meditation

Joyful living is my right. In love and thanksgiving I express my gratitude to God for His wonderful bounty to me by remembering that every time I fulfil a need in another person, I am showing in deed the gratitude I have in my own heart and mind. I now see that as I give myself over to gratitude for God-love and God-Law, my sense of well-being and expanded living brings me into a heavenly existence. I am now in heaven, and I intend to enjoy it and to consciously stay there.

Day 29

LAUGHTER AND HAPPINESS

Question. Is there really a secret key to success and happiness?

Answer. In Proverbs 3:13 we read: "Happy is the man that findeth wisdom and the man that getteth understanding." *The Science of Mind* textbook states: "Let us waste no further time looking for the secret of success or the key to happiness. Already the door is open and whosoever will may enter" (SOM 47:1).

Laughter is the surest sign of a carefree, confident, and happy soul. How often do you laugh from a sense of well-being, success, and a feeling of wholeness? Laughing people are happy people, even if the laughter is of short duration. How much more satisfying it would be if everyone laughed more! So why don't they? They would probably answer that no one can laugh while in desperate need or that no one can laugh while bowed down in guilt or while the body is racked with pain. All of this is true; but there is a way that can lead us away from hurtful feelings—a way that, if followed, would banish all distress!

Lack of laughter denotes a sense of insecurity. The pathway to a sense of complete security lies in a study of the Truth. One such way is through the Science of Mind teaching. We learn about the Divine Father of all; we are taught how to relate to Him, how to believe in His Almighty Power, how to accept His Love and Bounty, and how to welcome His Wisdom and Guidance in our day-to-day living. A life of total security gives us confidence. Confidence frees us to be able to be carefree and happy, and this releases the gift of bubbling laughter, which in itself has a healing quality. All negative influences fall away as we embrace our sonship and accept our inheritance.

Ernest Holmes tells us that "Prayer is essential to happiness" (SOM 178:2). Prayer is the action of knowledgeable thought by someone who understands and abides by the rules governing prayer. First, there must be a clear and precise understanding of what is wanted. Then comes a meditative quiet time when the ego mind has ceased its chattering and we are in a state of realization of the One to Whom we are praying and why. The 'why' is a reminder that nothing is impossible to God *if* there is sufficient belief in His ability to bring forth whatever is desired. The only proviso is that this desire be in accordance with the Nature of God—in other words, that it hurt no one nor deprive anyone of anything that may rightfully be theirs.

Meditating on the Omnipresence of God and His Divine Intention for Good to bless our life results in a conditioned consciousness of complete faith, belief, and trust. Belief is the absence of anxiety. An absence of all anxiety is that 'grain of mustard seed' that Jesus told us was essential.

Understanding what we are endeavoring to achieve results in the wisdom to use the power of our thought to bring forth great benefit. Wisdom and understanding can only bring great happiness—not a fleeting sense of satisfaction but an enduring and total surrender to the wise and loving Intention of God to answer prayer.

We must always remember that prayer, or treatment, does not heal our problems. It is the change of consciousness, which is a result of a prayer or treatment, that heals. Change your thinking to the positive and you change your consciousness to become unified with the Giver of All Good. When this is achieved, prayer is answered, security is assured, and happiness is the result.

As Dr. Holmes tells us: "Let us waste no further time looking for the secret of success or the key to happiness" (SOM 47:1). We can all think. We all have choice to control our thinking. Learning how to think in a positive, constructive way is not difficult—it only takes practice to establish a habit. An established habit becomes an automatic response, so that everything becomes easier.

Raymond Charles Barker says: "You don't take a leap of faith till you have built the bridge." The way to build that bridge is to study, absorb, accept, and practice. When we have built that bridge and taken that leap of faith, we have cultivated a deep belief and trust in the Presence of God where we are. He is only a thought away.

We begin to live a life in confidence and utter security. Now our laughter can be heard often, and others, curious about our happiness, question: "Why . . . what do you have? And can I learn too?"

Now we can laugh and be happy and teach others how to move into that wonderfully secure life.

Meditation

Practicing the Presence conditions my consciousness so that I see clearly and pray aright. Everything in my life is transformed, and I am transported to a state of constant happiness. My sense of confidence and total security enriches my life, and I am filled with laughter and freedom now and always.

Day 30

ACCEPTANCE

Question. In the story of the Prodigal Son we read that: "he came to himself." What is meant by that statement?

Answer. Until we find the pathway of Truth, we are all prodigals. In our ignorance of the power of thought and the existence of God-love and God-Law, we squander the 'sweets' of life that come to us over the years. We spend our substance in negative ways and often reduce ourselves to poverty, regretting the loss of our material gains.

We can be likened to the limb of a tree that has been severed from the source of its life. For a time it will exist on the nourishment within, but it will eventually wither and die. Unlike the severed limb, we can be reunited with our source. This is the true meaning of the story of the Prodigal Son.

The Prodigal Son, hungry, destitute, and miserable, declared in effect: "There must be something better than this," and he came to himself. The 'I am' of him was finally able to get through the layers of ignorance as he remembered that there is a God waiting for him to return. He turned away from negative living and took the first steps back to the loving Father.

While he was yet a long way off, his Father came to meet him and rejoiced!

We need to remember that the two greatest gifts that have been given to us are the ability to think and free will to be the author of our own thoughts. However, until we accept *in our heart* that our spoken word is the powerful directive to the Creative Law to act upon our words, our words will accomplish nothing. *Intellectual* acceptance is not enough, because without conviction that God-Law can be stirred, there is no belief in the Divine principle; there is a lack of trust.

It is not always easy to trust something we cannot actually see, or to trust something to happen without clear evidence that it will. Sometimes we need an example; and what better example in Spiritual Law than that which we already have?

Suppose we decide to repaint our house. We may choose a shade of green that is soft or strong. What do we do? Isn't it usual to mix blue and yellow in certain proportions to obtain the exact shade required? Does it ever occur to us that yellow and blue mixed together will not result in green?

It is the same with other natural laws that we use without question. Two and two always make four; positive and negative elements always produce electric power. These natural laws are trusted because from childhood we have witnessed and experienced their immutability. We trust them!

So it is with the Law of Mind. When this Law is properly used and understood, we shall learn to trust it implicitly. We shall learn to accept, trust, and use it without question. All we have to do is try it and prove it. Ernest Holmes says: "We must trust the Invisible, for It is the sole cause of that which is visible

113

. . . 'Things which are seen were not made of things which do appear' (Heb. 11:3)" (SOM 57:2).

There are many things we accept in our daily experience that would be better discarded. Too often we accept a state of ill-health as permanent; we accept shortage of money as a way of life; we accept loneliness as something to be endured. These and other negatives are things we believe to be true of us; and while this is what we believe and accept, surely the Law will provide more of that which we accept to be true of ourselves. God has given us Love and a Creative Law to use. He has also given us free choice. But we must direct the Law in the correct way for change to take place in our experiences.

In a way, we are all prodigals, often misusing our portion of the Good given to us by a loving Father. How often have we given what we could to our own offspring and watched it abused, wasted, and not valued? When we have misused the good we have been given, and then suffered the consequences, only then do we ask the question: "Why?" That is the time when we return to the Father's House and to the untold good He has for us.

How do we return to claim and accept all that the Father has for us? It is done by examining our thought patterns, assessing the degree of our faith in God's Love and Law, and thinking thoughts that reunite us with our Source.

It all depends upon what we decide to believe as true and accept about ourselves. Rich rewards await us for our diligence and tenacity. We practice watching the nature of our thinking, the tendencies we have, the degree of our confidence in God's loving givingness.

The Law can only be activated by our innermost conviction. If we are content to suffer, we shall continue to suffer. But if, however, we 'come to ourselves' and realize that something wonderful is waiting to be accepted, then nothing can prevent change from taking place.

When words are spoken as an expression of deep desire, they are empowered by God's love, which says: "Make your requests known unto me"; "Ask, believing, and you shall be given unto." We are dealing with a principle that cannot deny its own nature.

Supreme confidence in God-Law is the essential ingredient for successful prayer/treatment work. It is the first lesson to be mastered by the thinking man if he is to train his thinking ability to bring results. It is the ABC of inner consciousness. Just as words or sentences cannot be formed without a mastery of the alphabet, **thinking will not produce results without inner belief and conviction.**

It is done unto us according to our belief and acceptance.

Meditation

*The time has come for me to evaluate my choice of beliefs and acceptances. That which I would change **can** be changed. I now turn my mind and heart to the unchanging attributes of God. Health is available; abundance is awaiting me; peace, love, and success are mine for the acceptance. Already it is being done unto me exactly in accordance with that which I now accept for myself. And so I am blessed.*

Day 31

SECURITY FOR ALL TIME

Question. Is there a secret to living a fulfilled life? If so, what is it?

Answer. Ernest Holmes says: "The greatest good that can come to anyone is the forming within him of an absolute certainty of himself, and of his relationship to the Universe" (SOM 180:3). That is the message we have been emphasizing throughout these Daily Guides.

"This understanding will rob man of his loneliness and give him a sense of security which knows no fear, a peace without which no life can be happy" (SOM 180:4).

Dr. Holmes also says that: "There is no power in the universe but ourselves that can free us" (SOM 295:2). Free us from what? Ill health, poverty, loneliness, fear, guilt—all the negatives that do not stem from God. They are man-made through negative thinking, false beliefs, and ignorance of how to use God's gifts to free us from unwanted experiences. A clear understanding of our relationship to the Universe will guarantee security for all time.

In ordinary, everyday life, many things promote within us a sense of security. We feel it when, after a journey of hazards and setbacks, we finally step through the door of our home. Sitting in our own car gives a sense of security. It is like a friend; we feel safe. Our family life can provide security; it is a community where we belong and are accepted for what we are. Similarly, we belong to a Father God, a Divine Parent who can supply *all* our needs. All we have to do is to ask, believing in His mighty power to provide.

Human nature, lost in false belief, often places the blame for misfortunes on God. How ridiculous! The things of God are Absolute and forever. If ill-health were bestowed by God, no one could ever get better. If poverty were God-ordained, no one would ever rise above it. Loneliness, guilt, and fear would all be permanent if they were indeed inflicted by the Absoluteness of God.

But *they are not*, because people recover health every day. And there are those who shed poverty and move into greater financial security, while those living in fear and guilt are healed.

The secret is to see all negative happenings as passing and to replace false thinking with expectations of continued renewal and replacement.

The Law of Mind is like receptive soil: sow seeds and they will grow. If we want health, or any other good thing, we must believe that it is available. The seed sown *in steadfast conviction* will grow and mature. Since every thought is a seed, we must be constantly aware of what we are sowing. If they are seeds of discontent, greed, violence, envy, persecution, fear, loss, or lack, then we know that we are sowing poisonous seeds, which will certainly bear bad fruit.

"Think only on those things which are pure, of good report," said Paul.

When we learn *habitually* to sow positive seeds in the garden of our mind, we shall reap the positive results. And when we learn to trust our Spiritual Parent to such an extent that it would not occur to us to seek help from any other avenue, our security is certain and sure.

This is what Raymond Charles Barker means when he says: "Security is an inner acceptance of yourself as victorious over negatives." Within a heart and mind centered and entrenched in acceptance of the One Power and Presence, there can be no negatives.

"By the activity of our thought, things come into our life and we are limited only because we have not known the Truth" (SOM 295:1).

I would emphasize this quotation by saying that it is by the *habitual* activity of our *believing* thought that things come into our life.

"And ye shall know the truth, and the truth shall make you free" (John 8:32).

Meditation

Freedom to think is mine. The time has come for me to stop sowing seeds of unwanted plants. From now on, I watch my sowing and welcome wonderful experiences as they appear. I hold fast to the Truth, and as I remain steadfast in my relationship to the Whole, I experience security in all that I am, do, achieve, and receive.

A FINAL WORD

Neil A. Mence

The teacher asks the student: "What is the main thing that you have learned from these Daily Guides?" The student replies: "Basically, there are two 'facts' that have been revealed":

1. There is only God. This is what is known as the *Truth*.
2. God can only work *through* us. We do that by applying the Truth.

Let's enlarge upon both of these points.

1. **There is only God.** If there is only God, then all of God must be present everywhere, at all times. In other words, He is omnipresent (everywhere present), omniscient (all-knowing), omnipotent (all-powerful), and the one activity behind, in, through, around, over, and under everything that is. This is the allness of God.

Just as the sun continuously radiates, so does God forever radiate all the attributes, or characteristics, that form His nature. He must, therefore, be forever radiating ("Being," or demonstrating, if you prefer) as life, love, health, supply, wisdom, and every other good thing that one can imagine.

So this is the Truth—that God *is*. He is everything that we, each in our own mind, believe or perceive Him to be. This means that we are a part, or an individualization, of Him. Although He constitutes and embodies every part of us, we are, individually, but a part of Him manifesting in the visible world. That is why we may be described as being of Him, made in His image and likeness, children of God.

To state that God is All, Principle, Law, Truth, is to state a fact, just as gravity and electricity are facts. Facts, however, can do nothing by themselves. They have to be used; they have to be applied to a situation. We, as individuals, have the power to do this. That power is through the use of our mind. This leads us to the second point.

2. **God can only work through us.** God, as Law, cannot decide; He can only 'be.' Therefore it is up to each of us to choose what He should do for us, and this is done through our word, or thought. In other words, we direct God-Law, which gives to us through God-love. Whatever we think or say will happen *if we believe it*. This is the clincher! God can demonstrate only at the level of our belief.

Repeating an affirmation a million times a day may be effective after a while, because we have forced our mind to accept it. But if we believe with all our heart and mind and being that the words or thoughts that we are thinking are being acted upon by God *now*, then they manifest immediately.

It's not a matter of God doing more for one person than for another. It's entirely a case of: the more one believes, the more one will demonstrate. As we are told: "By their fruits ye shall know them." This means that everything in our life, including the things we don't like and that we may have labeled as negative, are a direct result of our conscious or unconscious belief. All through the Bible, and all through Truth teachings, we hear this same message: "It is done unto you as you believe."

One of my favorite passages in *The Science of Mind* textbook occurs in the chapter on Faith:

> Spiritual Substance is all around us, waiting to be formed. Thus we see what Jesus meant when he said: "And I say unto you, Ask and it shall be given unto you." The Law must work in compliance with our demand. The Divine Urge within us is God's way of letting us know that we should push forward and take that which is awaiting our demand. *If the good were not already ours in the invisible supply, it would be impossible for us to procure it in any manner.* "He openeth his hand and satisfieth the desire of every living creature" (SOM 157:3).

To sum up what we have learned in these Daily Guides: it is our job to:

- know the Truth (by reading, learning, and accepting),
- direct the Truth at whatever we want to accomplish in our life,
- believe that God is acting on our word, and
- accept that it is being *done now* (i.e. release and have no anxiety).

Let's apply this to a specific example. Imagine that I am seeking work or a new position. I follow the above steps by saying to myself, either silently or out loud:

1. There is only God. I know that He is all life, all love, all power. He is the only mind, the only substance, the only body. Since I am made in His image and likeness, He is always flowing (radiating, vibrating, expressing, pouring, etc.) through me into everything I think, say, and do. In Truth I am one with Him.

2. Since He is All, He is the position (or work) that I am seeking. It is the ideal position; it is all I have ever dreamed of in a position *(I should emphasize this point by adding as much description as possible to what I feel the ideal position would be)*. I know that I am guided to the place or position that is right for me. My talents and strengths are used to the full, and I am greatly appreciated. My success is certain and I am abundantly remunerated.

3. I know that you hear me, Father. I know that you always hear me. I give thanks for the right and perfect answer

to this request. I give thanks for the perfect position. I give thanks for answered prayer *now*.

4.   I now release my thoughts and words to Creative Law in complete trust and confidence. I am at peace, claiming a perfect outcome to this prayer. Thank you, Father. Thank you. I am receiving *now*.

The key to success is *realization*. Realization, Ernest Holmes tells us, means "an acceptance by the mind that a thought or condition is actual" (SOM 625, "Realization").

At all times, we need to guard against a sense of absence or loss, no matter how much the appearance may indicate it. *In Truth* we already have everything. When we believe that we have, our belief will enable it to come forth. This is the key to a successful treatment.

SUCCESSFUL TREATMENT

Norah Boyd

It is one thing to learn 'How To' word or speak a treatment so that it is indeed a scientific prayer. However, it is quite another thing to implant the necessary *energy of belief* in the *Invincibility of God-Law* in order to bring a satisfactory answer to such a prayer.

Theory is necessary in the first instance but, as Ernest Holmes says in *The Science of Mind* textbook: "One of the great difficulties in the new order of thought is that we are likely to indulge in too much theory and too little practice. . . . we only know as much as we can prove by actual demonstration" (SOM 51:1).

To encourage beginners in the application of Truth, I would like to share a few personal examples to show that scientific prayer does work if the rules governing its application are faithfully followed. Keep in mind that these rules include **Recognition, Identification, Steadfast Belief,** and **Release** of all anxiety concerning the outcome.

Many years ago, when I was widowed and left with a 19-month-old baby to raise on a pension of two pounds (approximately $3) a week, I had two real concerns. The first was that

124

my baby had no daddy and the second was whether I would have sufficient funds to feed, clothe, and educate my child.

At the time, I knew nothing of New Thought or Science of Mind, but I did have a deep faith in the Goodness of God. My daily prayer was: "Father, my baby does not have a daddy, and I don't know how to be one. I ask that whenever I need guidance, You will give me that guidance and help me to comply with it."

The years passed and, although it was a struggle, that child was somehow always provided for. In fact, one month when I had no money and couldn't see how I could feed my little girl, I took it to the Father. Four hours later, a friend called with a basket on her arm, saying: "Norah, I hope you won't be offended, but I have been shopping and have bought far more groceries than I need. I had a feeling you might welcome the extras, so I brought them along!"

It was enough to see me through the month until the next payday. From then on, there was always enough.

When my baby grew up and left home to marry, I felt very much alone. My only companion had been my daughter, Angela, and we had always done everything together.

I took my problem to the Father like this: "Father, I could sit and cry all day and waste my life; but when I meet up with Freddie [my late husband] again, I want him to be pleased with what I have done with my life since he had to leave me. I would like to meet someone, or a group of people, who think as I do." That same day I saw a small article in the local newspaper about a class on New Thought. I inquired, enrolled, and took all the undergraduate class work.

Finally came the day when those involved wanted to start a Church of Religious Science (which teaches Science of Mind). At that time, I was the only one ready to take the practitioner's course. I told my teacher that it was impossible: I had my job, my home, and an elderly mother to look after, and I simply could not just get up and leave them. Moreover, I had no money! My teacher advised me that there was a month-long accelerated practitioner class that was available, adding: "Do your treatment work!"

Standing at the bus stop on my way to work one morning, I heard a postman discussing his forthcoming trip to Canada. My immediate thought was: "A postman! How can he find enough money for such a vacation?" So in a very diplomatic way, of course, I asked him. He told me that he belonged to a travel club and that for just a few pennies a week the club arranged for members to travel on charter flights.

This was all fine, except where would I stay and what about finances? At that time, 50 pounds was all the currency that one was allowed to take out of the country. My teacher wrote to a friend who was a minister-in-training at the Institute of Religious Science in Los Angeles. He wrote back and said that as his tithe, he would be delighted to offer hospitality in his house at no cost whatever.

And so I went!

Upon returning to England I thought: "This is marvelous! I am now a qualified practitioner!" My balloon was soon burst, however, when I was told that the new church was being in-augurated and that it needed a minister. Since I was the only one qualified to take the ministerial course, I would have to take the training in Los Angeles—a two-year course. I was appalled! "I can't go . . . not for two years! It would mean giving up my job, leaving my commitments—and I *never wanted to become a minister!*"

My teacher said: "Do your treatment work!" The Institute wrote and said that as I would be an 'out-of-state' candidate, they would allow me to take the two-year course in one year!

Still resisting, I told my teacher: "I still won't have money for the fare." "Do your treatment work!" I was told.

On a shopping trip into town I met one of the future church board members and when asked if I was excited about my trip to America, I replied: "I don't know how I can find the fare. I shall have to turn in my insurance policy." My friend said: "You shouldn't have to do that . . . leave it to me." The result was that the board members all joined to supply my airfare.

On the plane I thought: "I must be mad! I've taken my last paycheck. I've left my home and family and I have no idea where or how I shall live once I get to L.A. Nor do I know how I will live when I return to England with no job to go back to. Moreover, I have no money and am not allowed to earn any while on a visitor's visa to the States." It was then that the thought came to me that "If I am going to teach this philosophy, I have to know beyond doubt that it is true and that it works, because I am resting my whole life upon it!"

When I arrived in the foyer of the Institute, I asked if anyone knew of possible accommodations. Someone said: "Our caretaker died two weeks ago and his widow might be glad to let a room." It was just around the corner (no traveling) and she was agreeable. A monthly rent for board and lodging was fixed but the question was how to meet it.

I approached one of the board members at the Institute and explained my problem. He said: "Leave it to me." The result was that a special scholarship was arranged whereby I would serve a certain number of hours each day as a practitioner in the Ministy of Prayer. Payment for this would defray the cost of board and lodging. I never saw any money but, when word got around that there was an English practitioner available, I was in constant demand, and the love gifts I received paid for all my incidental expenses.

Wonderful things happened to me — too many to relate here. Many times I would remember the injunctions: "Do the thing and the power will be given" and "Do your treatment work!"

Numerous success stories could be told by the many students I have taught over the years. Their good has come into being because they learned to ask, trust, and to 'let go and let God.' To 'let go' means to release all anxiety in the confident knowledge that the Creative Law does work and that we can trust God in all things *if* we obey the rules governing use of the Law.